After America: Australia and the new world order

First published in 2025 by Australia Institute Press
Reprinted in 2026

ISBN 9781-763-66213-1 (print)
ISBN 9781-763-66216-2 (ebook)

Published in Australia and New Zealand by
Australia Institute Press
www.australiainstitute.org.au

Cataloguing-in-publication data is available from the National Library of Australia

Proofread by Rod Morrison

Printed and bound in Australia by McPhersons Printing Group an accredited ISO AS/NZS 14001 Environmental Management Systems printer.

After America: Australia and the new world order

Emma Shortis

Australia Institute Press

Metaphors and historical parallels feel too cheap, too easy. The fanatical architects of Project 2025, the radical plan for Donald Trump's second presidency, had imagined their saviour inheriting "a world on fire".[1] In January 2025, as the man who described himself as saved by God so that he could Make America Great Again took the oath of office in the Capitol Rotunda, the other side of the continent was, quite literally, ablaze.

While Trump delivered his inaugural address in Washington, Los Angeles was experiencing what was predicted to be the most expensive "natural" disaster in American history, surpassing even the US$200 billion in damage caused by Hurricane Katrina in 2005.[2] Twenty-nine people died. More than 6,800 buildings were destroyed and nearly 23,000 acres burnt.[3] In winter. As Democratic Governor of California Gavin Newsom said at the time, climate change means that there are no fire seasons anymore.[4]

Our world is on fire. And now, Donald Trump is in charge of the most powerful country in it. The 47th President of the United States isn't interested in putting out fires. He's not just fanning the flames, he's busy lighting new fires of his own. Trump's recklessness and hostility to the old world order has direct, and immediate, economic, political and security implications for Australia. The consequences of Australian leaders failing to acknowledge, let alone adapt, to this new reality are hard to overstate. Put simply, just as Trump's willingness to buy Greenland, annex Canada and sell out Ukraine pose existential threats to those countries, his approach to Australia — and, more importantly, the response of Australian leaders — has the potential to reshape the present and future of this country, and our role in the world.

The America we thought we knew is gone. That America — our greatest friend and ally, our trusted protector, benevolent leader of the free world — never really existed. Trump, as he does with so many things, just makes that reality a lot harder to avoid.

Trump is both a product of American history and the worst of it reborn. It is both true that fascism has always been the chameleon of

American politics, and that Trump can give it a new and even more frightening form. It is both true that the United States never cared about respecting the international rules-based order, and that Trump is destroying whatever is left of it. All of this is historically consistent and logical, and yet nothing about what is happening is even close to normal.[5]

The America we thought we knew is over, and it isn't coming back.

For Australia, the question must be: what does *our* world look like, after America? How might we shape it for the better?

Right now, the world is a very dangerous place. The Trump administration is an active, direct threat to our security and to the security of our world. And to the extent that Australia hides behind our alliance with the United States, talks about our common values and attempts to make nice with a US President who has proposed ethnic cleansing in Gaza, and the forced acquisition of other countries, and is attacking America's traditional allies, including Australia, with tariffs and economic threats, this country is party to that threat.

It does not have to be this way. Australians

increasingly believe that it is time to re-think our relationship with the United States. Polling conducted by The Australia Institute in February 2025, only a month after Trump was inaugurated, makes that clear.

Nearly one third of Australians now see Donald Trump as the greatest threat to global peace — more respondents than chose either Vladimir Putin or Xi Jinping. Half of Australians think Donald Trump's election is a bad thing for the world — twice as many as think it's a good thing. Almost half of Australians also feel less secure since his election. And almost half of Australians are not at all confident that Donald Trump would defend Australia, or Australia's interests, if we were ever threatened. Given the choice, more Australians now would prefer that Australia pursue a more independent foreign policy over a closer alliance with the United States.[6]

Australians are listening when Donald Trump tells us who he is. Trump is an opportunity to rethink Australian, and global, security, because the threat he poses to that security is real.

In a world on fire, the threat Trump's America poses to Australia is literal and local.

Trump's dismantling of the international rule of law, his threats to invade other sovereign nations, his attacks on the constitutional order of the United States, the white-supremacist violence he is emboldening and enabling both at home and internationally, his fanatical commitment to accelerating climate catastrophe, all have immediate consequences for us.

As we watch, the few things about our alliance with the United States that actually make us safer, that help protect us from real and growing threats, are vanishing before our eyes. And the current American President is ideologically committed to speeding up that collapse and making it even more dangerous, for all of us. Climate change, he claims, is unreal. So too are its consequences. Drill baby drill is not just a slogan: it is a warning.

There are no fire seasons anymore. That means that American and Australian firefighters probably can't come to each other's aid anymore, as they have in the past. Australia and the United States, along with New Zealand, have been exchanging fire assistance and equipment for two decades. During the Black Summer bushfires of 2019–20, the United States dispatched four fixed-wing aircraft and about 270 personnel to Australia. In 2018, nearly 140 Australian and New Zealand firefighters spent a month on the west coast of the United States supporting firefighting efforts there. But by 2025, things had changed. As the ABC reported in January 2025, while California fire services struggled to contain the LA fires, "In the past, Australia has sent its own fleet of aircraft to assist with fires burning overseas, but with the country still in peak bushfire season and having already battled a number of blazes, it is on stand-by locally."[7]

But imagine how it might have gone if our two countries had been helping each other fight fires, as usual. Imagine how Trump would have weaponised the absence of any Californian firefighters or water bombers had they been deployed to Australia in January 2025. That was entirely possible. At the time, the east coast of Australia was also experiencing very bad fire conditions. In Victoria, the Grampians National Park had been burning for over a month. That fire took weeks to contain, with ongoing catastrophic conditions, and was still burning more than a week after Trump's inauguration. What if Australia had asked for, and received, some help from California before the US west coast caught fire, as we have done so often in the past? Just imagine how Trump would have used that, how he would have turned his wrath on Australia.

And it's easy to imagine something much worse. What might have happened had those American aircraft and personnel been denied to Australia in a local crisis? What would we have been left without? In the absence of significant investment in real national security — the ability to fight bushfires — we might well need help from American firefighting personnel and equipment again, if not this summer, then in the next. Or maybe in winter.

The Trump administration is busy doing all it can to make sure that we — and the rest of the world along with us — are going to need more help in facing the consequences of a world already on fire. The United States is not coming to save us. He has made that perfectly clear.

Just as he promised, one of Trump's first Executive Orders unilaterally withdrew the United States from the Paris Climate Accords. He immediately began the process of opening up more oil fields, which will dramatically increase US emissions. On day two of his presidency, he declared an "energy emergency" that will speed up the approvals process for new fossil fuel infrastructure. He rescinded vehicle emissions standards and President Joe Biden's "pause" on gas exports. He re-opened parts of the Arctic and the US coastline to oil and gas expansion. On Valentine's Day, Trump established the "National Energy Dominance Council" which will aim, according to the administration, to re-make the United States as a "net exporter of energy" and "the world's leading oil producer". All of this will amplify the effects of climate change, making the world a more dangerous place.

Frightening as this is, wringing our hands over the withdrawal of American action on climate change shouldn't blind us to the fact that the United States has never been serious about climate. President Joe Biden came to office promising to "restore" American global leadership on that front. In the 2020 election, "Biden ran for president on the most ambitious climate action platform of any major presidential candidate in U.S. history".[8] But his administration never reached such promised heights. In the first half of his term, Biden oversaw the passage of the *Inflation Reduction Act*, the biggest piece of climate legislation in American history. He committed the United States to a 50 per cent reduction in total emissions by 2030. Under his leadership, the United States rejoined the Paris Climate Accords, and he made first-time commitments such as promising Pacific Island states that America would continue to recognise their sovereignty and statehood even in the face of catastrophic territorial loss. According to *Vox* in July 2024, "When he leaves office in January 2025, Biden will be able to credibly claim that he has done more on climate change than any other president and has been one of the most consequential decision-makers in the world for the future of the planet."[9]

The problem is the bar is so incredibly low. The United States is "responsible for the largest share of historical emissions" in the world[10], and has consistently undermined multilateral climate negotiations and agreements. The global climate crisis itself has been largely driven by American capital. Under Biden's leadership, the United States increased oil production by 700 million barrels[11], gas by 140 billion cubic metres,[12] and never got close to achieving its emissions reduction targets.

But Biden's failures don't mean that Trump can't make things worse. He absolutely will. When the US President mocks climate science and the need to act urgently, the fossil fuel industry breathes a sigh of relief. The precise consequences of Trump's attacks on climate action, climate science and climate cooperation are difficult to forecast. But they are already cementing a bleaker future.

Even small and specific examples highlight the scale of risk and damage. In Trump's first month in office, his administration ordered the National Oceanic and Atmospheric Administration (NOAA) to pause all its international engagements. Those orders affected all of NOAA, including the National Environmental Satellite, Data, and Information Service (NESDIS). NESDIS, according to *Wired*, "relies on a wide range of international partners" to supplement its local data. That data "is essential not only to air transportation safety but also to combat drought, monitor coral reef destruction, and safeguard railway shipping carriers against dangerous weather"[13], which seems like it might be important.

There are myriad small examples that, added together, are bigger than the sum of their parts.

And they are happening in the broader context of the Trump administration's radical remaking of the United States and its role in the world.

In his first few weeks, Trump put a "pause" on all US foreign aid and effectively handed over the entire USAID agency to Elon Musk's "Department of Government Efficiency" or DOGE. Neither cared, of course, that it is illegal for the executive branch to do that; federal agencies can only be defunded or disbanded by an act of Congress. The dismantling of USAID is at once a constitutional crisis and a crisis on the ground. About 90 per cent of American foreign aid was unilaterally stopped.[14] America had been spending US$5 billion on food aid annually[15] and this move has left food rotting in warehouses.[16] Closer to home, from Papua New Guinea to Palau, Trump is ensuring the Pacific is further in peril. As one US expert put it, "closing down USAID will imperil our national security and put millions of lives at risk".[17]

At virtually the same time, Trump withdrew from the World Health Organization, indulging the ongoing Covid-mania of his supporter base. He stopped public health communication by the Department of Health and Human

Services (DHHS), the agency now run by Robert F Kennedy Jr. That department is also banned from international communication and cooperation. DHHS can't communicate with Americans about vaccinations or disease spread, nor cooperate internationally to support vaccine rollouts or mitigate the risk of another global pandemic.[18]

Trump's dismantling of key planks of the international order does not and will not stop there. At a press conference in early February, sitting beside Israeli Prime Minister Benjamin Netanyahu, Trump announced that the United States would "take over" the Gaza Strip and force Palestinians who live there to leave. Already subject to what Amnesty International has labelled a genocide, this would be an utter catastrophe for the Palestinians. It would also defy international law. Trump has committed the United States to supporting a policy of ethnic cleansing — a crime against humanity — and he has broken what was left of the international rule of law in the process.[19]

Then, in the Oval Office in February, Trump and Vice President JD Vance humiliated Ukrainian President Volodymyr Zelenskyy and all of America's traditional allies along with him. Trump is upending 70 years of global order, and it is not clear what will emerge in its place.

We know who he is

Understanding the threat this poses to us and the world means understanding who Trump is, and what he will do. It means understanding that there are no clean dividing lines between what happens in the United States and the role it plays in the world, as much as we might wish that were true. Our alliance with the US is not above presidents or prime ministers. We cannot separate Trump's domestic politics from the way the United States acts in the world. We must listen when Trump tells us who he is and what he is going to do.

He has been telling us since he descended that golden escalator in 2015. The most powerful man in the world's continued insistence that white men — the natural and rightful leaders of civilisation — cannot function in a society where women and non-white people are even visible. His talk of enemies of the state, vermin and immigrants poisoning the blood of the country is exactly what it sounds like.

More effectively than almost anyone else in the modern era, Trump reinforces and promotes fascist ideas of hierarchy of who is in and who is out, who is American and who is not, who deserves safety and security and who does not. Trump's promise, already on its way to being fulfilled, to implement the largest mass deportations in American history, embodies Italian philosopher Umberto Eco's observation, made 30 years ago, that "the first appeal of a fascist or prematurely fascist movement is an appeal against the intruders".[20]

That matters to Australia because Trump's imperial ambitions must be understood in this context. His threats to annex Canada, the Panama Canal, Greenland, his re-naming of the Gulf of Mexico, are all part of an aggressive imperial nostalgia that seeks to assert American dominance once more. Trump's vision for America as "a growing nation", violent, all-powerful, relentless and unforgiving, is a projection of American manifest destiny out into the world, and even beyond it. California, written off, is no longer the frontier of American historical imagination: Mars is. That is the scale of Trump's — and Elon Musk's — ego and ambition. Their vision is to conquer the world, the universe.

That is the magnitude of what we are dealing

with. So, how do we respond? What do we *do*?

Right now, in Australia, our leaders are doing much the same things that they have done for the last 70 years, since the signing of the Australia, New Zealand, United States (ANZUS) Security Treaty in 1951.[21] They are acting as though the America they are dealing with now, Trump's America, is fundamentally the same America we have relied upon for our security. They are acting as though what we have always done — supporting the United States no matter what and no matter why, to shore up the mythical security guarantee provided by the ANZUS Treaty — is what we should continue to do, even as the America we thought we knew disappears.

The inevitable fact is: the centrepiece of Australia's national security policy has been a strategy of pre-emptive capitulation, the immediate acceptance of American policy objectives as our own. Korea, Viet Nam, Iraq, Afghanistan — all of which cost Australia blood and treasure — were obedient acceptance of American interests.

Recognising that things are not the same as they once were requires bravery. It requires understanding and imagination. That is not what we have now.

An honour and a privilege

As soon as it was clear Donald Trump had won the presidential election in November 2024, Prime Minister Anthony Albanese expressed his congratulations. He said the Australian government would "work closely with the new Trump administration". He noted that "Our nations are bound by a history of shared sacrifice, a commitment to common values".[22] He didn't go into any detail about what "common values" we might share with Trump's America.

After attending Trump's inauguration in January, Foreign Affairs Minister Penny Wong reflected on what an "honour" it was to have "the privilege of attending the inauguration and being just a few seats back from watching the President speak".

At the end of January, Defence Minister and Deputy Prime Minister Richard Marles tweeted a photo of himself on the phone to newly confirmed Defense Secretary Pete Hegseth, with the *Australian* newspaper in front of him.[23] He was wearing cufflinks that looked like the Great Seal of the United States, a symbol of American sovereignty. What signal might the Minister have been trying to send?

A short while later, Marles flew to Washington to meet with Hegseth. As the Australian media breathlessly celebrated, Marles was the first foreign counterpart to meet the new Defense Secretary a man whose own mother called him an "abuser of women".[24] But Marles was suitably deferential. It was, he told Hegseth, "an enormous honour for me to be here and to see you in that role". Hegseth offered his own reassurance in return:

> We've got a lot to talk about on shared defence, our security priorities, the Indo-Pacific — the significant challenges and opportunities that you face there and we face — but Australia is the forefront of our alliance there and throughout the world, there's just no doubt about it. And it's strong and growing evermore, especially under President Trump's leadership

> in the first administration and now again, he has charged me with making sure this is as robust an alliance as we have in the entire world. So as far as defence is concerned; force posture, defence industrial base, joint capabilities cooperation and AUKUS, of course, are signature parts.[25]

This was the kind of reassurance, couched in the opaque jargon of defence, that the national security community in Australia are always so very desperate to hear. The (mostly male) experts who run defence policy in this country, cycling through the Defence department — and a few small but influential think tanks and universities, and the media that uncritically accepts their expertise — judged it all a spectacular success, of course. That was likely because Hegseth and Marles, and their teams, didn't talk about Trump's plans for Gaza or the defence repercussions of climate catastrophe, but they did talk about one of his favourite things: money. Australia's second-in-charge had come bearing the new administration a pretty tribute: $798 million for the US naval shipbuilding industry, the first down payment on a promised $5 billion non-refundable deposit on the AUKUS submarine pact.

Everyone involved breathed a big sigh of relief when Hegseth said, "The president is very aware [and] supportive of AUKUS".[26] Phew! Marles, for his part, said that the submarine deal — apparently the only thing that matters — was coming along nicely, and that he was "confident about its progress under this administration". As if to confirm that pre-emptive capitulation remained in play, Marles reaffirmed ANZUS as the cornerstone of both our defence and foreign policy.[27]

Three days later, Trump showed the Australian government just how embarrassingly misplaced that confidence in our alliance really was. On Air Force One, on the way to the Superbowl, Trump announced new, blanket tariffs on aluminium and steel imports into the US. In the predictably scripted Trump redux, the Australian government was sent scrambling. The Australian Business Council demanded immediate action. The opposition could barely disguise its glee, suggesting benevolently that they might send in former US Ambassador Joe Hockey or former Prime Minister Scott Morrison to Trump whisper — as if conservative deference were the only way to protect Australia from our closest ally.

To be clear, we are now at the point where the suggestion an ostensibly progressive Labor government should appoint an arch conservative, former prime minister as special envoy to Trump in order to ensure his continued favour is taken seriously. Apparently it didn't occur to anyone to point out what a ridiculous and irreconcilable betrayal of Labor values that would be. Nor about creating a dangerous precedent that Australia's ambassadors should be selected on their ability to fawn and flatter. Successful diplomacy is nearly always polite, but it is almost never based on appeasement. All that mattered was that Australia get a special carve out, exactly as the Coalition government under Malcolm Turnbull did so very cleverly last time.

So, the Prime Minister called the President. They had a "constructive and warm" phone call. Trump called Albanese a "very fine man", said some weird stuff about Australia buying planes because we're very far away, and let the Prime Minister say that a special exception was "under consideration".[28] Shortly after, Trump signed the Executive Order implementing the tariffs.

It was quite specific: no exceptions or exemptions. Not long after that, in the Oval Office with British Prime Minister Keir Starmer, when asked about AUKUS, Trump responded, "What does that mean?"[29]

What are we *doing*?

The entire ordeal was excruciatingly embarrassing. Whether or not Australia receives a carve out to exclude us from Trump's tariffs, things like this will keep happening. It doesn't matter how much they scrape and beg, how many billions of dollars we hand over. Trump doesn't care about us. Exempting us from a new tariff isn't a favour, it's a reminder of how vulnerable we are. Whether or not you think it was a good deal, Australia's Free Trade Agreement with the United States, signed 20 years ago, is clearly not worth the paper it's written on. Why would we think that the AUKUS pact, flimsier still, is worth any more? Or the ANZUS Treaty, for that matter? We're not special. No one is. The sooner our leaders admit that the safer we will be.

Trump and his surrogates have been loud and clear in their views that they will put themselves first. Not long after gracing the Australian Deputy Prime Minister with an audience, US

Defense Secretary Hegseth flew to Europe to speak to the Ukraine Defense Contact Group: a collection of about 40 of Ukraine's allies in its war against Russian invasion. He was there, he said, "to directly and unambiguously express that stark strategic realities prevent the United States of America from being primarily focused on the security of Europe".[30] The North Atlantic Treaty Organization (NATO) is in trouble. Trump's America is closer ideologically to Putin's Russia than it is to the United States' traditional European allies. But while Hegseth's comments still threw NATO into "disarray" things got much worse when Vice President JD Vance gave what *Politico* described as a "a U.S.-style MAGA, red meat speech" at the Munich Security Conference.[31] Vance told Europeans that the biggest threat to Europe was ... Europe. More specifically, European social-democratic values. The Trump administration has made it clear that it supports the resurrection of the far right in Europe, and that it does not care for maintaining the longstanding security guarantee provided by NATO.

If the United States is no longer going to be the primary guarantor of security in Europe, then they are not going to be Australia's, either. Unlike NATO, the ANZUS Treaty doesn't prescribe an explicit security guarantee from the United States, only a promise to "act", which could mean anything at all. To Trump, the chances are it would mean nothing. The United States would only ever come to Australia's aid if it were judged to be directly in the United States' interests to do so.

Donald Trump and his court are not concealing their contempt for the needs or expectations of their once close allies. But despite the clarity of Trump's message to Europe, the accepted wisdom among the senior ranks of Australian defence and foreign-policy wonks seems to be that Australia's expectation for the United States to keep us safe will have some persuasive power over the new regime.

It is hard to overstate the determination of those most responsible for Australia's foreign policy to find reassurance buried beneath the wreckage that the Trump administration has wrought. Some experts seem relieved that the Trump administration appears to be turning away from Europe, towards the Indo-Pacific, believing a greater US focus on the supposed threat of China will mean greater attention on our part of the world and, in turn, on us. But while the optimists may find comfort in Trump's abandonment of his European allies to focus on China, his preferred adversary, the costs and risks to Australia of such a US pivot attract little attention. Tying ourselves closer to the United States — Trump's United States — does not make us safer. It leaves us more exposed.

The longstanding bipartisan consensus in Australia is that we need our governments to cosy up to America, that we need the United States to perpetually increase its presence in Australia and in our region, if we are to maintain national security. According to this logic, we need our leaders to talk about common values with Donald Trump, which means being within eyeshot is an honour, and wearing cufflinks bearing the insignia of his nation, because it creates a guarantee of our safety. We need the Americans for protection, regardless of who is in the White House and how much they assault our common values or the international rule of law. There are no limits to pre-emptive capitulation.

The AUKUS disaster

The belief that Australian sovereignty is built on US foreign policy is why so many seem to believe that, even under Trump, Australia needs the AUKUS submarine pact.

AUKUS will be a disaster for Australia.[32] The rationale behind it is that Australian security can be purchased from the United States. But AUKUS forfeits Australia's autonomy, agency and sovereignty to the US. If it is ever implemented, it will do nothing to support Australian independence and do much to make us a bigger target. While Australia should be thinking about a post-American future, we are entangling ourselves more completely, and more expensively, than ever before. And despite the significance of the seismic shift in defence and foreign policy that the AUKUS submarines represent, the bipartisan support for the deal means neither the Australian Parliament nor the court of public opinion has had the chance to debate the decision.

AUKUS was conceived in secret and delivered in embarrassing pantomime. The most expensive purchase in Australian history never went to Treasury and was not even considered by the Department of Foreign Affairs and Trade. Many Pacific leaders learned about it in a newspaper. A lucky few got an early morning phone call.

The biggest change in Australian defence policy in decades and the biggest transfer of sovereign wealth in the history of this country was not debated by Cabinet, in the House of Representatives or the Senate. Voters were not advised or consulted. A few years later, in October 2024, the US Congressional Research Service, which provides independent advice and information to US Congress, put it rather drily: "There is little indication that, prior to announcing the AUKUS Pillar 1 project … an analysis of alternatives (AOA) or equivalent rigorous comparative analysis was conducted to examine whether [AUKUS] would be a more cost-effective way to spend defense resources".[33]

AUKUS is supposed to equip Australia with up to eight conventionally armed, nuclear-powered submarines, through the support of the US and the UK. When the deal was first announced by then Prime Minister Scott Morrison in September 2021, there wasn't a plan to achieve that. All the pesky detail was left to Morrison's successors. The federal Labor Party, desperate to avoid being wedged on national security in an executive decision that undermined usual party process, committed itself to the deal. Losing an opportunity to take a considered look at AUKUS, perhaps by sending it for a proper independent review, the new Labor government capitulated and attempted to retrofit Morrison's political stunt into credible policy.

Perhaps they did the best they could with what they had to work with. The problem was that they didn't have much. The plan they developed, unfortunately dubbed the "Optimal Pathway", was not announced until March 2023[34], 18 months after President Joe Biden and UK Prime Minister Boris Johnson announced the deal alongside "that fella down under".[35] The Optimal Pathway, though, isn't optimal, and nor is it a pathway. It is long and extremely complicated, with significant risks of failure built into each step.

With some notable exceptions, the national-security wonks don't like it when non-experts stray onto their turf. But you don't need to be an "expert" in defence policy, materiel or even nuclear-powered submarines to understand the risks and the dangerous assumptions that abound along the Optimal Pathway. And, even as our eyes glaze over at the opaque defence jargon, it is worth identifying those risks as clearly as possible — even if we are working off the assumption that the highly unlikely on time and on budget delivery of the AUKUS submarines would enhance Australia's security and independence.

The plan to make AUKUS work involves three stages. The first is an immediate upgrade to Australia's current fleet of Collins-class submarines, extending their life until the arrival of the promised nuclear-powered replacements. The second is that from the 2030s, Australia will acquire somewhere between three and five Virginia-class nuclear-powered submarines from the United States. The third is that from the 2040s, the SSN AUKUS — British–Australian -designed, Australian-built, AUKUS-class nuclear-powered submarines — begin to enter service. The first is scheduled for the early 2040s, followed by one new submarine delivered every three years, which means the eighth and final boat would not arrive until the mid-2060s.[36] For decades Australians have been told by successive governments that we can't take major steps to tackle the risks of climate change due to the long-term time horizons and high up-front costs but, when it comes to the imagined risks of foreign invasion, costs and timeframes are no barrier.

The first stage of the path towards AUKUS is the "LOTE" or "life-of-type extension" of the Collins-class submarines which involves an almost complete overhaul and rebuild of the current fleet. Work on the restoration of Australia's vintage submarines is unlikely to begin in earnest until 2026.[37] The overhaul, even if it goes entirely to plan — a vanishingly rare achievement in defence logistics — almost guarantees that Australia will have fewer operational submarines in the immediate future. This will affect crew training, experience and numbers, which will have flow-on effects for the second and third stages of the AUKUS pathway.

The second stage — the part where we get second-hand American Virginia-class nuclear-powered submarines — is probably worse. This stage is explicitly based on the assumption that the US will have surplus submarines and, in turn, that they can spare the oldest members of their fleet. There are already serious questions about the current rate of submarine construction in the United States.[38] Why would any future US administration risk undermining its own fleet capabilities by handing over command of some of its most elite assets to Australia?

The current AUKUS legislation has a get-out clause for future US presidents, who can decide not to hand over any nuclear submarines if the US believes they need them for themselves. It gets worse. The latest iteration of the AUKUS deal allows the US and the UK to pull out altogether if they decide the deal prejudices their own defence. Even if the United States did hand over spare Virginia-class submarines, which is unlikely, any such handover would come with conditions. And if it did happen, it's important to remember that the Australian Navy has no experience operating or maintaining nuclear-powered submarines. Under the Optimal Pathway, it has less than a decade to learn (while simultaneously managing the Collins upgrade).

There's more. In stage three — the bit where

the actual AUKUS submarines are supposed to be designed and built — Australia will be beholden to the British shipbuilding industry, which is in an even worse state than the American one. It, too, is plagued by delays, extreme cost blowouts, and operational issues. To be clear, the UK is yet to even design the AUKUS-class submarines that Australia says are critical to our defence over the next century.[39]

The Optimal Pathway means the UK will now have to manage three separate programs: completing the construction of the already late British Astute-class submarines, designing and building replacements for the British Vanguard submarines, and designing and building the new AUKUS boats. Australia has already committed a non-refundable $4.6 billion to clear "bottlenecks" in the UK submarine industry (that's in addition to the nearly $5 billion already committed to the US industry that we'll never get back). All going well, the newly designed AUKUS subs will then be built in Australia, where there is no existing trained labour force or infrastructure.

Even *if* the program is successful, which is the biggest if in the history of Australian defence policy, Australia will then have to crew, operate and maintain three separate submarine classes simultaneously as the Virginia- and AUKUS-class submarines gradually replace the renovated Collins class. And we will have to manage the nuclear waste. And some unspecified amount of nuclear waste from our friends in Britain and America. And we have no detail on when or how much.[40]

Easy.

The difficulties of designing, building, crewing and maintaining three submarine classes at the same time creates enormous financial and operational risks for Australia. But these risks are arguably small compared to the strategic, sovereign and political risks that this stunt involves. While hundreds of millions of dollars will be spent on project managers to help ensure that AUKUS stays on the Optimal Pathway, the real risk to Australia comes if we stay this course. The reality is that AUKUS will cede Australia's decision-making autonomy to the United States.

The US, and any other country paying attention, knows how completely AUKUS straps Australia to the mast of US defence policy. In April 2024, Kurt Campbell, Deputy Secretary of State in the Biden administration, candidly observed that AUKUS means Australia is "locked in now for the next 40 years".[41] Campbell also described Australian and US military forces as now having a "deeper interconnection, almost a melding".[42] Australian and US military capability has long been described by the Australian defence set as, ideally, "interoperable" — capable of deploying together in combined or joint operations. But under AUKUS, that is changing into something much deeper.

In mid-2022, Defence Minister Richard Marles boasted of Australia's "move beyond interoperability to interchangeability".[43] Interchangeability implies a level of seamlessness, where equipment, personnel and command are integrated and swappable. In August 2024, another US official, Admiral William Houston of the US Naval Nuclear Propulsion Program, gave a small preview of what that could mean. Houston revealed that Australian sailors would soon make up 10 per cent of the crews on US-flagged Virginia-class attack submarines in the western Pacific.[44] That might not sound like a big deal, but it is.

Australia has followed the United States into almost every war it has fought since the end of the Second World War, no matter where it was fighting or why.[45] It is, as current opposition leader Peter Dutton has said, close to "inconceivable" that a future Australian government would not continue that historical trend: to do anything different would require a massive historical break.[46] It is still theoretically *possible* that some future Australian government might say "no" to joining American military adventurism. Under "normal" circumstances, an Australian government might think twice about supporting a US invasion of Greenland, to give one not entirely hypothetical example. They might still go, but any support could be carefully calibrated, and there would still be, theoretically, enough room to say "no" without destabilising the alliance and Australian security. Yet again, a suitable piece of real estate in Alice Springs would come into its own. Under AUKUS, Australian involvement in American-led wars is reaffirmed as the default setting.

Future Australian governments could try to "opt out" of US wars, but it is very difficult to imagine an Australian prime minister pursuing, or a US government accepting, a delay to US submarine deployment to withdraw 10 per cent of the crew. In that scenario, an Australian government would have to not just to say "no", but to actively delay American war mobilisation. It is equally hard to imagine an American administration, set on war, accepting such a delay. And it beggars belief that the US would leave itself beholden to a foreign power, even an ally as close as Australia, for the operation of a core naval capability.

AUKUS is a deal for the biggest transfer of funds in Australian history. Made in secret, with highly unlikely outcomes both in the intermediate and long term, the deal ties Australia to American foreign policy even more closely that in the past. And anyone who might have some questions about that, is, according to Minister for Defence Industry and Capability Delivery Pat Conroy, an agent for "appeasement".[47]

That is the calibre of the conversation we have about foreign policy in this country. It would be funny if it weren't so dangerous. AUKUS, and our alliance with the United States more broadly, will only make us less secure. Even before Trump won back the White House, the world had become a more dangerous place. Trump's predecessors, and Australia's unquestioning support of them, share a significant portion of the blame for creating a more unstable world.

The sky is dark

President Joe Biden liked to say that the United States, and the world, faced an "inflection point" in history.[48] He was engaged in a "battle for the soul of America", which seemed to be, along with the rest of the world, teetering on the brink. Undoubtedly, we sit at a dangerous point in our history, and it is easy, and tempting, to fall into cynicism and despair. At the end of January 2025, as Trump was assuming power, the Bulletin of Atomic Scientists moved the Doomsday Clock from 90 to 89 seconds to midnight — the closest it has ever been. The Clock, established in 1947, aims to act as a warning about just how close we are to destroying ourselves and our planet. And according to the Science and Security Board of the Bulletin, we are frighteningly close to doing that. As board members explained in early 2025:

> Because the world is already perilously close to the precipice, a move of even a single second should be taken as an indication of extreme danger and an unmistakable warning that every second of delay in reversing course increases the probability of global disaster.[49]

Biden was right to say that America, and the world, sit at an inflection point. But Biden, and governments around the world that failed to understand and respond adequately to those real risks, bear much of the blame for how we got here. Many American voters feared more of the same from Democrats more than they feared Trump. Biden's presidency left the world a more dangerous place. Understanding that, and how these failures have facilitated Trump's return to power, is critical to understanding how we might change course.

Biden always saw himself as a foreign policy president, as a leader who could make America, and the world, more secure. He prided himself on his foreign policy experience. During his time in Congress, he spent 12 years as either the Chair or the Ranking Member of the Senate Foreign

Relations Committee. The Obama White House, leaning on his credibility as a (safely male and white) elder statesman, claimed that the then Vice President had "played a pivotal role in shaping U.S. foreign policy".[50]

Born in the first year of America's involvement in the Second World War, Biden always had a misty-eyed view of the United States and its role in the world. He lived through some of the greatest unresolved contradictions of American history: the first use of nuclear weapons; the drafting of the UN Charter; the Civil Rights movement and the assassinations of John F Kennedy, Dr Martin Luther King Jr, and Robert F Kennedy; America's wars on Korea and Viet Nam. Then the optimism occasioned by the end of the Cold War and the brief interregnum of the 1990s, when a victorious and virtuous United States seemed to have vanquished the forces of tyranny to the dustbin of history.

Despite its manifest shortcomings, Biden's conviction that the United States remained the best country in the world never dimmed. Biden's version of American exceptionalism is more generous than some others', but it remains just that. On election night in 2020, when he had finally achieved his lifelong dream of winning the presidency, Biden reassured the American people that despite everything they had endured for the past four years, "I believe at our best, America is a beacon for the globe".[51] He never wavered in that conviction — if anything, it strengthened over time. Three years later, speaking to the American people from the Oval Office after a visit to Ukraine, Biden said that he "felt something I've always believed more strongly than ever before: America is a beacon to the world, still, still".[52] The then President even went so far as to quote the Clinton administration's Secretary of State Madeleine Albright, who described the United States as "the indispensable nation". Like Trump, Biden believed the world couldn't persist without a strong US.

When he was elected, Biden promised to restore the United States to that rightful, central place in the world, as the bulwark of global democracy, a place full of division and contradictions but where nevertheless, better angels prevail. Biden was a student of American history[53], and he wanted to be another Franklin D Roosevelt, both re-maker of the American economy in favour of working people and the victorious but benevolent leader of the free world. But he became, in the end, more of a Lyndon B Johnson, a one-term president who oversaw a disastrous foreign policy program that undermined his domestic agenda, paved the way for a generational victory for the American right, and left the world a more dangerous and unstable place.

Like LBJ, Biden was always torn in two, pulled between the progressive wing of his party on economics and domestic politics and a much more conservative and ruthless view of the United States' role in the world. Like LBJ, Biden was drawn to the idea that the United States had existential enemies that it simply had to contain; for LBJ it was the Soviet Union, and for Biden, it was China. The need to win a "great power competition" with China became one of the very few, if not the only, areas of bipartisan consensus in the United States during the Trump era. That meant, like Trump 1.0, Biden attempted to marry his domestic economic agenda, through investment in American manufacturing, with a Cold-War era mindset that perceived China as an existential security threat. So, Biden continued Trump's first term agenda of aggressive economic policies towards China, leaving Trump's tariffs in place, and even adding some of his own. In 2022, the Biden administration implemented a broad-based export ban on semiconductor chips and other advanced technologies. At the same time, he oversaw passage of the US$280 billion *CHIPS and Science Act*[54], which aimed to revive US semiconductor production and reduce what was widely understood as a dangerous overreliance on overseas (read: Chinese) technology. It was clearly an attempt to strangle Chinese industry and revive American technological dominance, and to walk a thin line between progressive, pro-worker policies at home and brutal *realpolitik* internationally, a kind of presidential doublethink. Biden's primary responsibility was clearly to Americans, and, as he saw it, primarily to American workers.

But Biden, perhaps unwittingly, never succeeded in bridging the gap between leadership at home and leadership of the world. While legislation like the *CHIPS and Science Act*, and other signature laws such as the *Inflation Reduction Act*, delivered huge investments in the American domestic economy, they were not enough. Biden's liberal faith in the goodness and rightness of America meant that he tinkered at home and continued long-standing trends abroad. He made some Americans' lives materially better but did not alter the underlying structures of American inequality that gave rise to Trump, and he restored a version of American leadership to the world that Americans themselves had long ago stopped supporting. He couldn't out-Trump Trump, and he couldn't let go of his vision of America as a shining beacon to the world. In the end his lack of domestic ambition delivered much of middle America to Trump while his foreign policy kept millions of progressive voters away from the ballot box altogether.

America and the world

No president can dictate what happens in the world during their time in office. But they can control how they respond. Much like his approach to China, President Biden's response to the Russian invasion of Ukraine in February of 2022 could not escape the confines of old ideas about the United States' role in the world. He rightly condemned Putin's war of conquest; he said all the usual things about freedom, liberty, democracy. He was, after all, always a Cold-War warrior. Biden pledged American support, but always stopped short of committing American forces; his primary responsibility was to keep Americans safe, and as much as he stuck to the trends of American global leadership, he was never going to risk direct confrontation with Russia. But Biden lacked the imagination to find a new approach and fell back into old American habits. His administration provided significant funding and weapons to Ukraine. By 2025, the United States had given $65.9 billion in military assistance, and the equivalent of around US$31.7 billion from Department of Defense armament stockpiles.[55] Under Biden's leadership, the United States, as it has done so many times before, provided aid and funding to those fighting an oppressor, a great power that was also widely regarded as a direct threat to American hegemony. But it never provided enough for the Ukrainians to comprehensively defeat that power, lest that draw the United States in too far. It spent billions of dollars to maintain a horrifying status quo, without ever doing the real work of peacebuilding.

And then, after the horrific attacks on Israel on October 7, 2023, we all watched Joe Biden's United States enable a retaliatory genocide against the Palestinian people. Biden's response to those attacks, and his ongoing support for the Israeli government's vastly disproportionate reaction, exposed the worst of American global "leadership", an experience from which that leadership might never recover. It also irrevocably destroyed Biden's own legacy. The President's initial response to the October 7 attacks was predictable and necessary, and a reflection of his genuine compassion. Biden described the attacks as "a terrible tragedy on a human level. It's hurting innocent people — seeing the lives that have been broken by this, the families torn apart. It's heartbreaking".[56]

Joe Biden has always been good at grief. That was, unusually, a big part of his personal appeal to the American people. His own life is marked by tragedy and mourning, which he genuinely turned into a reflection of his country's long mourning of lost promise. In 1972, the young Joe Biden had just been elected to the Senate when his wife and daughter died in a car accident. And he had always presented himself as the heir to the Kennedy legacy, as the embodiment of a nation mourning the devastating loss of a promised new world (to the point where he was forced out of contention for the presidential nomination in 1988 after plagiarising a Bobby Kennedy speech). Biden melded political mourning with the personal, so much so that he was known in his time in politics as an accomplished deliverer of eulogies for his colleagues. Fittingly, one of his last official acts as president was to deliver a eulogy for President Jimmy Carter. Death always haunted Biden, but at his best, that meant he was beautifully human; it meant he loved wholly and unconditionally.[57] By 2020, when he was running against Donald Trump, Biden embodied a kind of personal and national compassion. He was the grandfather everyone wanted, who promised to love America back to itself. That man was lost in Gaza. Biden's human compassion was superseded by his promise, on October 7, that "the United States stands with Israel. We will not ever fail to have their back".[58] That promise stayed in place, no matter what the Israeli government did. Even as it became clear that the Israeli response was destroying Gaza, as appalling images of children and babies flooded social media, Biden barely flinched. Biden's compassion suddenly seemed conditional; he extended it to Israelis in a way that he would not, and could not, for Palestinians. Estimates vary, but under his leadership, the United States provided around US$17.9 billion in aid to Israel in the year following the October 7 attacks.[59] That support is historically consistent: according to the Council on Foreign Relations, since 1946, the United States has provided, in current terms, over

US$300 billion in aid to Israel, the vast majority of which takes the form of military aid.[60]

Since October 7, that aid has been used, with Biden's support, to pursue the destruction of Hamas. That is an understandably appealing but completely unrealistic objective. And it has meant that with the Biden administration's vocal and unwavering support, Israel has turned Gaza into an uninhabitable wasteland. Close to 50,000 Palestinians have been killed, perhaps a majority of them women and children and non-combatants. Biden attempted to negotiate a ceasefire with an Israeli government, led by Benjamin Netanyahu, which had nothing but contempt for the American president.[61] It was always clear that Netanyahu was waiting Biden out, hoping that Trump would return to office and that he would once again have the support of the American far right, free of even the meekest constraints Biden had placed on him. The waiting paid off. And it paid off, at least in part, because Biden's support of that same government did so much political damage to him at home.[62]

It's worth noting here that in Australia, the government's response to the horrors unfolding in Gaza has been largely supportive of Israel, leading to university campus protests and, as early as November 2023, the home affairs department warning the government of a sense of anger and betrayal in some communities.[63] Australian complicity in this response contributed to the undermining of the international rule of law that Trump is now escalating.

In the United States, Gaza mattered to Biden's electoral chances. By appearing to remain indifferent to the horrifying images coming out of Gaza, Biden destroyed his own image of a man of compassion, a man who really saw and heard his people. To many Americans — and particularly a core part of the coalition that supported Biden's run for the presidency in 2020 — the hypocrisy was unbearable.

In Washington on 25 February 2024, a young man set himself on fire in front of the Israeli Embassy. Twenty-five-year-old Aaron Bushnell's "extreme act of protest" was a rejection of "complicit[y] in genocide".[64] Bushnell later died from his injuries. This young man's horrific death was indicative of the depth of feeling in the United States. Young people felt deeply betrayed by the Biden administration's unwillingness to make an intervention to stop the indiscriminate slaughter of Palestinians, particularly children. They were, and still are, confronted every day by the horrors of what American bombs, missiles and guns are doing to the people of Gaza. They were begging their president to help. Biden appeared either unable or unwilling to see or hear. Two days after Bushnell's protest in Washington, Michigan held its primary. In a state with a significant proportion of Arab-American voters — a state that was central to Biden's defeat of Trump in 2020 and would clearly be a critical battleground again in 2024 — 100,000 voters described themselves as "uncommitted" instead of supporting the Democratic nominee.[65] The message could not have been clearer. And the party ignored it.

Biden's betrayal was even more glaring because he had appeared, at times, to understand Americans' fatigue with war and American global "leadership". It was Biden who, after two decades, over US$2 trillion and over 240,000 deaths, finally ended the longest war in American history when he withdrew the United States from Afghanistan.[66] The withdrawal, though widely panned by the press, at least indicated at new possibilities and a recognition of the failure of that kind of American "leadership" of the world.

But the reality is that Biden's arrogance — both his own personal arrogance in his refusal to step aside for new leadership, and his arrogant faith in American goodness — risked global security and the very democracy he thought he alone could save. And the Australian government supported him unconditionally, giving him credibility while failing to act like a real friend should and warning Biden of his folly.

When Biden's personal arrogance was finally punctured by that disastrous debate performance in mid-2024, the national arrogance lingered in his party. Even with the promise and renewal of a young and vibrant candidate in Kamala Harris, the Democrats could not manage the contradictions of peddling some "progressive" policies at home while also running an empire abroad. That wasn't necessarily obvious when Harris assumed the candidacy. The enthusiasm around her was real, and it was infectious. Generational change in America, a new "brat" era, suddenly seemed a lot more possible than it had mere days before. Perhaps Biden had, unwillingly, built that generational bridge he had promised in the 2020 campaign.

A new (new) hope

It was easy to get caught up in the hype. In the week leading up to the election, I went to a Harris rally in Charlotte, North Carolina. It might well be the script from a writer searching desperately for meaning and symbolism, but when I got into the Uber that would take me to the rally at a stadium outside of town, Taylor Swift was singing that she was going to write your name, baby, in a blank space. It was too perfect. The energy at the rally itself was warm and wholesome. Women easily outnumbered men, a very rare experience at a political event that isn't specifically for or about women. Young Black women mingled and laughed with older white women who might have been Massachusetts Senator Elizabeth Warren's older sisters. The whole event was almost flawlessly organised and executed, with musical acts including a revamped Jon Bon Jovi joined by two Black artists who were far better singers than he. Harris was immaculate: warm, funny, responsive to the crowd, hitting her lines perfectly. A few days later, I followed her to Philadelphia for her last rally on the night before the election. I didn't get in — the line was too long.

Harris' loss the next day was as predictable as it was devastating. Her supporters had known the night before. It was clear from late in the evening, as Trump outperformed Harris in the rustbelt states. The mostly young Black students at her election night rally at Howard University in Washington had started trickling out by about 11 pm. I returned there with them the next day, to see Harris give her concession speech. She spoke beautifully to a subdued but captivated audience. Perhaps the most striking thing about that audience — the thing that will stay with me forever — is just how many of the young women were not crying. It was not that they didn't know what Harris' loss meant, and not that they weren't frightened or devastated by it. It was that they had always known. Those young Black women especially, in the words of sociologist and *New York Times* columnist Dr Tressie McMillan Cottom, "know our whites".[67] They know, have always known, how America treats them. Harris' loss to a man like that was just further proof of the contempt their country has for them. Harris, like them, had to hold herself together rather than give into despair. As Harris ended her speech, she left those young women with this:

> There's an adage a historian once called a law of history, true of every society across the ages. The adage is, only when it is dark enough can you see the stars. I know many people feel like we are entering a dark time, but for the benefit of us all, I hope that is not the case. But here's the thing, America, if it is, let us fill the sky with the light of a brilliant, brilliant billion of stars.[68]

The light hadn't gone out, but as Harris left the stage, it dimmed. On the long walk out of Howard, I met another woman who was there by herself. A young elementary school teacher from New Jersey, fresh out of college, she asked me if I wouldn't mind if she walked with me for a while. She was frightened, I think, and, like me, didn't particularly want to be alone in that moment.

I was glad to have someone to talk to. We chatted for a while. She was, she said, a little bit relieved. She had realised, when Harris lost, that being perfect didn't matter. Harris was as close to perfect as she could be; she had the qualifications, the experience, she was across the detail, she was beautiful, articulate, funny, she displayed just the right level of emotion, and she wore all the right clothes. And it didn't matter. Aspiring to perfection was pointless. She still lost. To a man like that.

By all the usual measures, Harris ran a good campaign. Given she'd had so little time, her ability to rally support, and particularly to fundraise, was remarkable. Of course, there's no such thing as a perfect candidate because there are no perfect humans. In another time and in other circumstances, Harris might have been the one to do it. But that would have required something other than perfection; it would have required a recognition of just how far the political ground has shifted in the United States, and a shedding of the particularly American arrogance that had undone Biden and would undo Harris. Whether it was inability or unwillingness to distance herself from Biden, the results were extremely damaging. That kind of radical change was, clearly, beyond Harris and her party. Harris did not appear to share Biden's personal arrogance, but she did embrace the Democratic Party's ideological arrogance about the United States' role in the world. As long as Democrats failed to recognise that arrogance and its consequences, they were destined to lose. The consequences of that failure are catastrophic for the United States, and for the world.

During the election campaign, hints of that grim future were everywhere. They were there at that same rally in North Carolina, the weekend before the election. The enthusiasm that day in Charlotte was a little surreal; the way Americans treat politicians like celebrities — cheering and whooping for even a state candidate for Commissioner of Agriculture — is pretty weird. When Harris appeared on stage, the crowd went wild, cheering all her well-delivered stump speech lines. But the way they cheered for her strangely specific policy proposal for addressing price gouging in supermarkets, which would clearly do almost nothing, felt forced even by American standards. In my notes, I wrote: "imagine cheering that loud for a price gouging law. Lol". The idea that such granular tinkering was the kind of thing Americans — even rusted-on Democratic supporters like those there that day — wanted or needed was never believable, I think even to the people cheering along.

That point was pretty clear a few minutes later when some young people in the middle of the crowd unfurled a banner protesting American complicity in the genocide in Gaza. It was remarkable that they had gotten it in, given the level of security. The crowd immediately turned on them; the hostility was palpable. Harris reacted with grace, telling the audience that democracy was complicated. But the crowd jeered and booed, and the protestors were dragged out. Harris said some half-hearted things about a ceasefire and then pivoted almost immediately to talking about small business. The remaining crowd, relieved, went back to cheering. Meanwhile, the joy had been badly undermined by the aggressive drowning out of young people protesting a war, just as it had for the whole campaign. Harris later said that Generation Z was "impatient for change". It was already evident she wouldn't give it to them, and that they knew it.

Just as Harris spoke of economic progress and specific policies that were supposed to help with the cost of living, the Labor Party's 2025 Australian election campaign is proclaiming the benefits of its legislation while households are struggling to pay electricity bills and mortgages. Voters may not always pay much attention to legislation in parliament, but they do notice when politicians tell them something that doesn't match with their reality.

In the United States, the foreign policy arrogance Harris inherited from Biden was not offset, as it was in the first half of Biden's term, by progressive economic promise. At one point, Biden had recognised the link between human security and prosperity at home and abroad, and a healthy democracy. But then he lost it, and all his successor had to offer was some repair work at home and more of the same internationally. In a sad twist, Harris offered a return not to the misty-eyed leadership of Biden's global beacon but a doubling down on hard-edged American power. Harris framed herself as the establishment candidate on national security, completing the long morph of the Democratic Party into what former Senator Bernie Sanders' foreign policy advisor Matt Duss now describes as "the party of war".[69]

Harris offered worse than nothing on Gaza. She instead promised that under her leadership, the United States would have "the most lethal military in the world" (as if it didn't already). She laughed about her personal possession of firearms, joking with Oprah Winfrey about how anyone breaking into her house is "getting shot".[70] The (perhaps unintended) contempt that she showed for a critical organising part of the Democratic base in young people against gun violence was, presumably, supposed to be offset by bringing "swinging" Republican voters, those mythical centrists, into the Harris camp. The same strategy sat behind the recruitment of the Cheneys, human embodiments of Republican conservatism, as campaign surrogates. The Democratic Party positively crowed about the endorsement of former Vice President Dick Cheney — a key architect of the disastrous War on Terror — wheeling his support out at every opportunity. To whom, exactly, was that meant to appeal?[71] If the election result is anything to go by, precisely no one.

Both the Biden administration and the Harris campaign made claims for their liberal credentials in domestic policy while perpetuating

American empire overseas. While their country has the worst gun violence in the developed world and their military is the most lethal, they expected voters to accept that inaction and appeasement at home and abroad were enough. Only 64 per cent of eligible voters attended a ballot box.[72] People who might have voted Democrat stayed away, leaving the field wide open for Donald Trump to claim the anti-war mantle, once again. Trump could see what Biden, Harris and the Democrats could not; Americans are exhausted by war and violence and are devastated by the human, economic and security disaster caused by the forever wars. That version of the empire makes no sense to them because they see no tangible benefits.

That failure allowed Trump to assemble a narrative and a loose coalition of support for his apparent anti-war stance that became central to his appeal and eventual return to the White House. Trump's promise to end the forever wars, and to not start any new ones, his insistence that the current wars devastating the Middle East and eastern Europe and the threat of a new one with China would all be ended or avoided with him in charge is appealing, even if, like much he says, it is a lie.

President for peace

Donald Trump is not anti-war. He is not an isolationist.

Trump *loves* violence. He has made, as Australian writer Don Watson observed, attending Ultimate Fighting Championship (UFC) matches a symbol of his cultural power.[73] He describes violence — like the home invasion and attack on former House Speaker Nancy Pelosi's husband Paul — with visible relish. He talks about blood, in particular his own blood and how much of it streamed down from his ear when he was almost killed by an assassin, constantly. He once described Australia's alliance with the United States as "sealed in blood".[74]

Trump extends that violence out into the world. He is often described as the first American president since Jimmy Carter not to start any new wars. It is possible to argue that on a technicality, depending on how you understand "starting" wars in the context of American empire. And, as usual, any war that the US starts would be a war that Australia fights … whether we like it or not.

During his first administration, Trump oversaw the military deploy "the mother of all bombs" — the most powerful non-nuclear weapon in the United States' arsenal — on Afghanistan. The bomb targeted an ISIS stronghold in the east of the country, near the Pakistani border. The weapon was developed by the US military at the end of the 2000s, for use in "psychological operations" in Iraq, according to military officials. The idea was that the bomb, which detonates before it hits the ground to create an enormous blast zone, "would rattle Iraqi troops and pressure them into surrendering or not even fighting".[75] Great plan. After it was tested in 2003, according to *The New Yorker*, "the Pentagon ordered a legal review to ensure that the device wouldn't be deemed an indiscriminate killer under the Law of Armed Conflict".[76] The US military didn't end up using the bomb in Iraq, and there was no strategic justification for its use on Afghanistan. As the United States should have learned in Viet Nam, that kind of aerial bombardment might feel dramatic and satisfying, but it doesn't work against a committed insurgency. However, it did have a strong psychological effect on the President. Trump loved it. It made him feel powerful. As he put it, surrounded by men in uniform, "this was another successful mission". He claimed, of course, that there was a "tremendous difference" between the way he was handling the military compared to the Obama administration. Two years after that "successful operation" in 2019, Trump sat next to Pakistani Prime Minister Imran Khan and said that "I have plans on Afghanistan that, if I wanted to win that war, Afghanistan would be wiped off the face of the Earth. It would be gone".[77] That is one way for a president to "end" a war he promised would be over on his watch, except he never ended it. The forever war continued into Biden's term.

Trump didn't end wars. He nearly started new ones. In fact, Trump's first administration was marked by dangerous brinksmanship. In January 2020, Trump ordered the extrajudicial assassination of Iranian Major General Qasem Soleimani. Head of the Iranian Quds Force, a branch of the Revolutionary Guard, Soleimani effectively ran Iran's proxy wars in the Middle East, but both George W Bush and Barack

Obama had declined to target him due to the risk of such an assassination provoking direct conflict with Iran. Trump, evidently, thought it was worth that risk, or didn't care. Soleimani was killed by an American MQ-9 Reaper drone Hellfire missile "pre-emptive strike", along with six Iraqis. Trump said that Soleimani had been killed because he was planning an "imminent attack" against American targets. A former Obama administration Middle East official called the killing "for all practical purposes, a declaration of war".[78] Iranian supreme leader Ayatollah Ali Khamenei said that "a forceful revenge awaits the criminals who have his blood ... on their hands". For days, no one really knew if the situation would deteriorate into outright war. American security hawks, long obsessed with pursuing regime change in Iran, were unrestrained in their delight. In Australia, the prospect of joining the United States in another war reared its ugly head. The Morrison government, which had not been informed of the operation, wouldn't be drawn on whether it would follow the Trump administration into a war. But it was perfectly clear that it would have.[79]

Trump openly mused about wiping countries

off the map, and about using nuclear weapons to do it, and he always had tacit Australian support. Before what was described as his "love affair" with Kim Jong-un, the North Korean dictator, Trump frequently played with (nuclear) fire. In 2018, in response to a speech by "little rocket man", Trump tweeted that "I too have a Nuclear Button, but it is a much bigger & more powerful one than his, and my Button works!" It was a perfect distillation of Trumpism, desperately juvenile, and yet deeply serious in the danger it posed to the world.[80]

This same man is back in charge of the biggest and most dangerous nuclear arsenal on the planet. As Dr Ruth Mitchell, one of the founding members of the Nobel Peace Prize-winning International Campaign Against Nuclear Weapons, put it: "the existence of a world leader like Trump ... really calls the lie to the idea that there are any good hands for nuclear weapons". With Trump's prolific brinksmanship, as Mitchell observes, "The only reason we haven't all been blown to smithereens and aren't currently in a nuclear winter is literally luck".[81] And now our luck is held in Trump's (very large) hands once again.

In the lead-up to Trump's election victory, it became a tired truism to say that a second Trump administration would be worse than the first. But it is true nevertheless, and circumstances will deteriorate further; Trump has already shown that to be the case. Those focused, rightly, on Trump's direct threats to the institutions and practices of American democracy kept pointing out, this time around, the guardrails are gone. The slightly saner heads that kept Trump from actually going to war with Iran, or strategised to stop him doing something like ordering a strike on China in his last days in office, are gone. Calling those people the "adults in the room", though, lets them all off the hook. Some of Trump's former staff like James Mattis or Mark Milley — both of whom later condemned Trump — still enabled him. And they still share many of the dangerous, hawkish views that motivate the worst of American military interventionism. And it also implies that the people around Trump now aren't adults. But they are, and they know precisely what they are doing. And it is to these adults that Australia has so closely tied ourselves with AUKUS.

None of those people — with the potential

exception of Tulsi Gabbard, Director of National Intelligence — are actually against war. They might be against certain types of war, and certain types of people dying in them, but they generally see war and conflict as inevitable. Trump himself isn't against wars, he's just against *losing* them. Luckily, in his mind, he doesn't lose. Trump and the people around him channel a Reagan-era idea about American wars. It is motivated by the belief that the United States lost wars like the one in Viet Nam not because those wars were ill-conceived, or because the United States fought them so badly, but because the United States was catastrophically undermined by internal forces and conspiracy. This idea suggests that in Viet Nam, for example, the United States lost because of left-wing betrayal at home. It wasn't described as "woke" then, but the assumption is the same. In this mindset, an America unleashed, led by powerful men like Trump, can't lose.

Trump's Defense Secretary, Pete Hegseth, continues to espouse this idea. The US military, according to Hegseth, has been so weakened and undermined by wokeism that it has forgotten how to fight and win wars. Hegseth wants to restore a "warfighting mentality" because, as he told NATO leaders in February 2025, "We can talk all we want about values. Values are important ... But you can't shoot values, you can't shoot flags, and you can't shoot strong speeches. There is no replacement for hard power".[82] Hegseth's own "values" extend to not being that keen on the Geneva Conventions, the rules that limit the conduct of war. In his book, *The War on Warriors*, Hegseth wrote that American troops "should not fight by rules written by dignified men in mahogany rooms eighty years ago", as if those rules had never stopped Americans from slaughtering innocent civilians. Nevertheless, according to Hegseth, "if we're going to send our boys to fight — and it should be boys — we need to unleash them to win. They need them to be the most ruthless. The most uncompromising. The most overwhelmingly lethal as they can be".[83]

Hegseth has had Trump's ear for quite some time. During his tenure as a talking head on Fox News, Hegseth was able to convince Trump, mostly through the screen, to pardon three US servicemen, two of whom were serving significant jail terms for murdering innocent civilians in Iraq and Afghanistan. Australia already has a poor record on war crimes based on soldiers' actions in Afghanistan. If this is the force with which we are developing interchangeability, does that mean an increased flouting of the Geneva Conventions with our allies?

A total disregard for the international rule of law permeates the second Trump administration. Those rules have never really applied to the United States, which has refused to sign up to many international treaty arrangements, such as the International Criminal Court, but the second Trump administration has taken that to a new, more dangerous level. Trump has always made it clear that he cares a lot less about certain kinds of people dying than others, and it is no accident that he is surrounded by people with the same mentality. The precise consequences of that for the world are hard to forecast, but we received a preview in the Trump administration's "plans" for the Middle East. Trump has said that the US should "own" Gaza and that it should be thought of as a "big real estate site". It might be a real estate deal to Trump, similar to his 1980s developments in New York that explicitly locked out Black tenants to make room for white ones. But to the people he has surrounded himself with — men like Hegseth and Vice President JD

Vance — it is much more than that. American support for Israel, like American support for Trump himself, has always been underpinned by the white evangelical movement. In early 2024, before Trump tapped him to be the vice presidential candidate, I heard JD Vance articulate this religious motivation clearly at a conference in Washington hosted by the Quincy Institute for Responsible Statecraft. It was clear then just how dangerous Vance is. Coverage of the election campaign, in which he didn't perform particularly well, obscured his considerable political skill, but on that day, Vance held the room in the palm of his hand. He was persuasive, and warm, and has an extraordinary ability to make the most radical, violent ideas sound like common sense. If he ever comes to Australia, just watch the media and politicians fall over themselves for him. In that speech in Washington in May 2024, Vance outlined his vision for what he described as a "foreign policy for the middle class". By "middle class", Vance meant white, Christian Americans, and, when it comes to Israel, as Vance said:

> a big part of the reason why Americans care about Israel is because we are still

> the largest Christian-majority country in the world, which means that a majority of citizens of this country think that their savior, and I count myself a Christian, was born, died, and resurrected in that narrow little strip of territory off the Mediterranean. The idea that there is ever going to be an American foreign policy that doesn't care a lot about that slice of the world is preposterous because of who Americans are.[84]

This combination of ideas about "hard power" with evangelicalism is not new to the United States.[85] What is new is who is in power, and how committed they are to wielding it.

Global re-alignment

Perhaps one of the more surprising manifestations of this newer version of a historically familiar combination is Trump and the MAGA movement's alignment with Russia. One might expect the heirs to Ronald Reagan to be hostile to the United States' former existential enemy. But Vance's logic on Israel, Hegseth's on hard power, Trump's love of powerful men, and their misogyny and white supremacy, all speak to a close ideological alignment with Putin's Russia. To them, Russia today is a successful ethnostate: a largely white country that has successfully suppressed and cowed minorities, especially LGBTQI+ people, and put women where they belong, in their homes waiting for their boy soldiers to return from the battlefield in glory. As key architect of Trumpism Steve Bannon put it: "Putin ain't woke".[86]

Trump's apparent "anti-war" stance on

Ukraine, and his promise to end that war on "Day 1", are motivated by this ideology, and not by his love for genuine, lasting peace. When Trump did start signalling about bringing that war to an end in February 2025, he did it by starting talks between the United States and Russia, to which Ukrainian President Volodymyr Zelenskyy wasn't even invited. At the time of writing, the Trump administration is making noises about territorial concessions that would reward Putin for the invasion and represent an unacceptable loss to Ukrainians of sovereign territory. But Trump doesn't care about the sovereignty or freedom of other nations. As made clear by his support for the insurrection and his hostility to courts of law that dare to challenge him, he doesn't even care about American democracy, let alone democracy elsewhere.

What Trump does care about is American primacy. He cares about ensuring that the United States remains the world's greatest power, able to do whatever it wants, whenever it wants. And that mindset means perceiving any possible challenge to that power, even if it is a question of economic equivalence, as an existential threat that must be defeated. That is how Trump's Cabinet, and a large and powerful part of the movement that brought him to power, view China. Trump himself might not be inclined to wage war with China, but a large part of his Cabinet is. And as we know, who has Trump's ear matters a great deal to what he does.

The reason Secretary Hegseth is so worried about the state of the American military, so preoccupied with its lethality and its apparent turn away from "warfighting" as a core mission, is because he sees China as a clear and present danger. China, he has said, is building the military capability to defeat the United States. Those are the "stark strategic realities", that Hegseth told NATO leaders in February would "prevent the United States of America from being primarily focused on the security of Europe". The United States will instead turn its focus to "a peer competitor in the Communist Chinese with the capability and intent to threaten our homeland and core national interests in the Indo-Pacific".[87] While Hegseth spoke about the need for "deterrence", his language, and that of the Trump administration more broadly, demonstrates a hunger for large-scale warfare.

Hegseth's views are reflected in the Heritage

Foundation's Project 2025, a program Trump cleverly downplayed during the election campaign, but which now holds a central place in his administration. Project 2025's *Mandate for Leadership* describes China as "America's most dangerous international enemy". In a clear echo of neoconservatives' love for regime change, it argues that the overwhelming priority of the Department of Defense should be defeating the threat of the Chinese Communist Party.[88] In the *Mandate*'s foreword, the former President of the Heritage Foundation, Kevin Roberts, argues that "Economic engagement with China should be ended, not rethought". Imagine the consequences for the Australian economy if the Trump administration asked Australia to do the same?

Project 2025's chapter on the Department of Commerce suggests "strategic decoupling from China". While Trump may have mused about nuclear arms control, the *Mandate*'s prescriptions for achieving this total defeat of the United States' "primary enemy" include dramatic expansion of the size and scope of the United States' nuclear arsenal. That should happen, it argues, alongside a reduced force in Europe (already hinted at by Hegseth), combined with an increase of 50,000 personnel stationed largely in the Asia Pacific. Imagine where many of those troops are likely to be based.

The *Mandate* doesn't make clear how that recruitment would happen, except to suggest that "all students in schools that receive federal funding" should be required to complete the military entrance examination. It does not seem like a stretch to suggest that the architects of Project 2025 — now key figures in the Trump administration and the broader ecosystem of ideas that informs it — are flirting with the revival of the military draft. That isn't exactly an idea that could be described as a "anti-war" or even "isolationist".[89]

In fact, none of this — significantly increasing the United States' global military footprint, negotiating with Russia, taking over Gaza, confronting China — could be described as isolationist or dovish. The Trump administration might be withdrawing from international agreements and treaties, but it's not withdrawing from the world. Trump doesn't want to hide from the world, he wants to stomp all over it. He is normalising the idea of the United States invading other sovereign nations such as Greenland, Panama or even Canada, and taking their territory, by force, for the United States. Trump loves violence, he loves the idea of making America bigger, of conquering the planet. He could easily be convinced to start a war, if he thought he could win it at a reasonable cost. And even if he doesn't, he has no interest in building genuine peace or security, for anyone.

The key questions for Australian defence planners and those shaping our foreign policy is simple: do they think the Trump administration's approach to China will make Australia safer and our economy stronger? If not, what are they going to do about it?

Enablers and collaborators

There is plenty of opposition to Trump's abhorrent ideas in the United States and outside it. Right now, that opposition lacks cohesion and is divided on how best to respond. Much of the loose coalition of organisations and people opposed to him is busy trying to put out the spot fires Trump is lighting: fighting him in the courts on his hard-line immigration policy, supporting those on the ground affected by those policies, looking for avenues to fight against his and Elon Musk's slash-and-burn approach to federal agencies and employees. All of that is necessary, but it is transactional. They are responding to the Trump tactic of letting off distraction grenades to make everyone run in all directions.

And to date, the Democratic Party — the most obvious platform on which to build coherent resistance to Trump — does not know how to respond to him. Many of what we might label "establishment" Democrats who supported Harris' policies, and who have failed to understand either her loss or even Hillary Clinton's nearly a decade ago, are busy blaming the left for Trump's victory. They are fighting among themselves, not recognising or using their power.

In February, *Axios* reported that senior Democrats were "pissed" that grassroots organisations were mobilising constituents to call their Democratic representatives, asking them to do more to resist Trump. "Some Democrats," *Axios* reported, "see the callers as barking up the wrong tree given their limited power as the minority party in Congress." The report suggested that Representative Hakeem Jeffries, House Minority Leader and heir apparent to Nancy Pelosi, was "very frustrated" that grassroots groups "are trying to stir up a more confrontational opposition to Trump".[90] Viewed from outside, the Democrats' early plan, if we can call it that, appears to be to wait Trump out. That approach is reflected in Australia, too, where the second Trump administration seems to be understood as something volatile and dangerous but ultimately temporary. The idea that this storm will pass and that soon Trump will be gone, is startlingly common.

Trump himself might well go, but who and what will he leave behind? What damage will he do to American democracy, democracies around the world, and the way countries see their allies in that time? Will Trump's second term really be limited to four years? What happens if the man who is only a heartbeat away from the presidency suddenly finds himself in the Oval Office?

Trump is dismantling the rule of law at home and abroad, the climate is collapsing, fascism is rising and billionaires are pillaging. Meanwhile, bolder strategic options exist, both within the US and in countries like Australia. And recent history suggests that a lack of political bravery may well be the most dangerous thing for centrist and progressive political parties. Trump's enablers and collaborators aren't just in America. They can be found in governments all over the world.

Establishment parties and incumbent governments are struggling to adapt to new realities, and they are being punished for it. The American presidential elections might have taken up most of the airtime and attention, but Trump's victory against an incumbent president was only one in a long line of defeats for democratic governments globally. In 2024, depending on how you do the maths, about half the population of the world — somewhere between two and four billion people — went to the polls. While direct comparisons are not always helpful, there just might be some lessons for an incumbent Australian government to draw from those results.

In Britain, Prime Minister Rishi Sunak and the Conservative Party were doomed to lose. The electorate had had enough with 14 years of Tory rule and the disastrous execution of Brexit. In the end, on the appropriately symbolic fourth of July, American Independence Day, the Tory government faced its worst defeat since the 1800s. Under Keir Starmer, UK Labour finally returned to power. But that victory wasn't so much Starmer's victory as Sunak's loss. Labour won its biggest parliamentary majority since Tony Blair stormed to victory in 1997, but it did so with a smaller share of the vote than when it suffered a devastating loss in 2019 under Jeremy Corbyn. Some of that is the result of the UK's anti-democratic first-past-the-post system, and some of it is because the conservative vote was split by Nigel Farage's Reform Party. Either way, it does not bode well for Starmer's Labour government. That government, like the Albanese government here in Australia, is a timid one. It promises only tinkering, focusing on stability at the expense of genuine reform. UK Labour's vote share sits at about 33.7 per cent. At the same election, Greens and independents increased their share; in fact, a record of five independent candidates were elected. Labour's vote share was arguably damaged by voters rejecting Starmer's positions on Israel and immigration, which, in a familiar pattern, pandered to the right. As Steve Howell wrote in *The Nation* shortly after the election, Starmer

> got lucky and won by a landslide because the opposition was divided. If there is a realignment on the right, with Farage rampant, continuing to pander to their agenda will only drive more people into Farage's arms. If Starmer doubts this, he need only take a look across the Channel to France, where Emmanuel Macron's austerity and concessions to bigotry have proved electorally fatal.[91]

While "fatal" might be a little dramatic, there is no question that incumbent French

President Emmanuel Macron is in a great deal of political trouble. In June 2024, the centrist President dissolved the National Assembly and called snap elections. Given the electoral map, it was assumed that the French far right would storm to victory. But at the last minute, the left assembled itself into a loose coalition, the New Popular Front, and secured a remarkable 188 seats in the Assembly, beating both Macron's centrist Ensemble alliance's 161 and the far-right National Rally's 142.

Macron, instead of interpreting these results as an indication that he should perhaps tack left rather than right, appointed a right-of-centre ally in Michel Barnier to the Prime Ministership. Barnier's party had secured a whopping 48 seats and he assembled a government from the centre and the right, supported by Macron. With the conditional support of the far-right National Rally, Barnier's government embarked on a program of austerity. By December, Barnier was gone, losing a vote of no confidence, and Macron was busy ignoring the National Assembly. Macron managed to have François Bayrou, from his own coalition, form government and pass a budget in February

2025. The situation remains precarious. Macron has until 2027 to turn things around.

His counterpart in Canada, Prime Minister Justin Trudeau, also facing the perils of incumbency, announced that he would step aside as party leader in early 2025. Trudeau's Canadian Liberal Party, thrown into disarray by the Trump administration and facing significant public frustration with a housing crisis and rising inequality (sound familiar?), was staring down defeat in elections that must be held by October 2025. When Donald Trump announced that he would be imposing blanket tariffs on all Canadian exports, Trudeau reacted as most other democratic leaders had in similar circumstances, not unlike how the Albanese government reacted when Trump announced those blanket tariffs on steel and aluminium. Trudeau called Trump, and then he flew to Mar-a-Lago to dine with the president-elect. They had a "very fine" conversation over what Canadian media described as "one of the most important dinner dates Justin Trudeau has ever secured" and Trudeau returned to Canada with precisely no guarantees about anything.[92] Trump, predictably, then doubled down, "joking" about Trudeau being the "governor" of the "51st state", musing about incorporating Canada into the United States. But then something happened. Perhaps unexpectedly, the Canadians stopped playing nice. Trudeau hit back with some retaliatory 25 per cent tariffs of his own. Canadian social media users started calling for boycotts on US goods, and Trudeau encouraged consumers to "choose Canada". Canadian crowds started booing the American national anthem at hockey games. And between December 2024 and February 2025, Trudeau's Liberals, even without a new leader, jumped from a dismal 16 per cent in the polls to 37 per cent. This increase in voter support was described as "insane" by one Canadian polling aggregator.[93] It's almost as if standing up to an autocratic bully is appealing.

What's left of democracy

With a way to go before the Canadian election, polls this far out aren't always a clear indication of the eventual result. And incumbent governments like Trudeau's, as with Macron's, Starmer's, and even Albanese's in Australia, are contending with the surging far right, each a local manifestation of Trumpism. Across the world, the far right is capitalising on the erosion of genuine, human security, on the effects of austerity and climate change, the rise in inequality, the human impacts of housing crises, and the general sense that things aren't getting better, that governments don't have anything real to offer. Many of the problems, which are the drivers of the anger and frustration that drives their electoral support, are the same problems for which they have no solutions.

The erosion of voters' faith in government's ability to effect change has been perpetuated by decades of neoliberal erosion of the institutions of the state, a cycle that the far right is seeking to entrench. While many progressive political leaders seem content to say "I told you so" when it comes to the failures of privatisation, deregulation, free trade and trickle-down economics, the far right are blaming woke DEI policies and stoking anger. That is the point of Elon Musk's DOGE, to burn everything down and leave worse than nothing in its place.

Undermined trust is reflected in how people feel about their governments, and about how democracy functions. In 2024, research by Pew found that across 24 countries surveyed, 59 per cent of respondents were "dissatisfied with how their democracy is functioning". Forty-two per cent agreed that "no political party in their country represents their views". And just shy of a three-quarters majority at 74 per cent thought "elected officials don't care what people like them think".[94] In media coverage, results like this are often framed as declining support for democracy itself, but that isn't it. These results reflect people's expectations about what they think democracy is. Democracy thrives on high expectations. Trump and his cronies such as Elon Musk want to bury those expectations. They are dismantling American democracy and undermining faith in the state to consolidate their power.

It is possible to fight back, and to raise expectations about what governments can achieve to materially improve people's lives. Doing so is crucial to the health of democracy. And the evidence that it works is clear; the Albanese government itself has shown this is true. In early 2024, after years of pressure, the Prime Minister announced that the government was scrapping the Morrison government's Stage 3 tax cuts, even though they had promised to keep them. Until that announcement, it had been widely assumed that breaking an election promise would be political self-sabotage of the highest order. That argument was continually made by people inside the government and pundits, even though the tax cuts were a policy disaster that would have overwhelmingly benefitted the top 10 per cent of income earners during a cost-of-living crisis, while delivering nothing for people on the minimum wage. The government got brave, and announced that it was scrapping Stage 3 in favour of a fairer policy delivering an extra $84 billion to low- and middle-income earners over the next

10 years and doubling the tax cuts for Australians on the average income. These changes are better for 85 per cent of taxpayers and for the Australian economy long term. Funnily enough, the finger-wagging about broken promises dissipated pretty quickly. It turns out that people break promises all the time in response to new circumstances, and that voters appreciate governments responding to their needs. Polling by The Australia Institute showed that Australians across the political spectrum and income ranges were strongly in favour of the new policy.[95] When a government delivers policies that benefit Australians across the board rather than just the richest minority, voters respond. One of the most progressive Australian tax changes in decades is popular.

Stage 3, though, is a lonely example for the Albanese government. It has mostly engaged in tinkering; with issues like housing and childcare, it has been extremely reluctant to take on meaningful, structural reform. Ahead of an election, the Australian Prime Minister is promising not the kind of progressive change offered by the Stage 3 changes, but more of the status quo. Interviewed on Sky News in January 2025, Albanese's pitch to the Australian people was continuity: a government that "has been stable, has been orderly, has been united". Who cares?

With Stage 3 the exception that proves the rule, in policy terms, the Albanese government resembles what Kamala Harris was offering the American people: a recognition that things aren't great for a lot of people, coupled with a response that feels inadequate. Technocratic, overly complicated policies laden with jargon and admonishments about the things that aren't possible. And over all that hangs duplicity and hypocrisy. Both Harris' Democrats and Albanese's Labor Party, for example, readily recognise the threat climate change poses to all of us. But their policies don't come close to risk mitigation of an existential crisis.

During the presidential election campaign, Harris steered away from climate change except to promise to cause more of it. She promised not to ban fracking, and talked up the benefits of the Biden administration's gas expansion.[96] In Australia, the Albanese government visits the Pacific and talks about standing shoulder to shoulder with our Pacific family, talks about emissions reductions, and then approves new coal mines and gas expansion. Australia remains the world's third largest fossil fuel exporter. But the government collects more money from HECS repayments than it does from the petroleum resource rent tax.[97] These things don't add up. And people know it.

In the United States, this hypocrisy and timidity has undermined trust in governments and opened space for an already emboldened right wing. Current opposition leader Peter Dutton clearly sees Trump's victory in the United States as an opportunity. Dutton is busy importing Trump's style of retail politics to Australia. This kind of political exchange isn't new; our two countries have always been very good at bringing out the worst in each other. Our "common values", after all, are at least partly based on a shared foundational history of dispossession, genocide and colonisation.[98] During his first term, Trump described that shared history quite clearly: "Our two countries," he said in 2019 alongside then Prime Minister Scott Morrison, "were born out of a vast wilderness, settled by the adventurers and pioneers whose fierce self-reliance shaped our destiny."[99]

In his second term, Trump has continued his gleeful erasure of Indigenous people's cultures and history. In his inauguration speech, Trump foreshadowed that specific and deliberate erasure when he outlined plans to re-name the United States' tallest mountain, Mt Denali — the Athabaskan name for the peak — Mt McKinley. At the same time, Dutton's opposition started attacking First Nations Welcome to Country ceremonies as "waste" and "divisive". They went so far as to name Senator Jacinta Price "Shadow Minister for Government Efficiency" in a clear emulation of Musk's DOGE. And in the lead-up to the federal election, billionaire Clive Palmer took his Trump wannabe act even further than before, announcing he was creating a new party called the "Trumpet of Patriots".

How deeply embarrassing. And it might not work in Australia — polling suggests there is a limited a constituency for Trumpism here, and even if there were, compulsory voting means that importing Trump's tactics of mobilising parts of the electorate won't work here as it does in the US. But we can't draw dividing lines between domestic politics and the rest of the world, and especially not between our politics and American politics. Especially not in a world of interchangeability. They are interrelated. How can a Labor government successfully rebut Dutton's amateur Trump policies if they aren't willing to fight back against the real thing? If Australia isn't brave enough to take on Trumpism abroad, how can we do it at home?

Rethinking Australian "security" after America

The America we thought we knew is not coming back. America in 2028 will be different, perhaps worse. And Australians, along with much of the world, are eager for something different. In polling conducted by The Australia Institute in February 2025, 44 per cent of respondents agreed that it is in Australia's interests to pursue a more independent foreign policy.[100] The way we think about our relationship with the United States, and our role in the world, is changing and changing quickly.

Those who insist that we can carry on as we always have, that we can just ride Trump out, or that we have to remain close to his version of America because that is the way we have always ensured our "security" are leaving the field open to bad-faith actors, making our world even less safe.

Proponents of the status quo also have

a shallow and ungenerous understanding of what "security" really is.

Supporters of the AUKUS deal, and blind supporters of the US, typically exaggerate the threat to Australia of countries like China while deliberately obscuring the risks to our security and the security of our region if we unquestioningly follow the US. Those risks include miscalculations or deliberate provocations of war between great powers. They also include threats such as catastrophic climate change, another global pandemic, nuclear annihilation, and the breakdown of the rule of law. But to our current leaders, those real threats don't appear to matter, because our current understanding of security doesn't consider so-called "soft" issues such as environmental catastrophe or the collapse of international law as genuine threats.

The Australian government *says* that it considers climate change a threat to regional stability and international security. The 2024 Australia–Tuvalu Falepili Union, for example, committed both countries to "enhancing their partnership to promote and protect the Parties' shared interest in each other's prosperity, stability and security, including by responding to current and emerging security challenges, such as climate change". The Union also recognised that "climate change is Tuvalu's greatest national security concern". But that rhetoric is not matched by action. Australia's subsidies to fossil fuel producers and major users totalled $14.5 billion in 2023–24. That number is an *increase* of 31 per cent on the recorded figure in 2022–23.[101] Since 2022, the Federal Environment Minister has approved 10 new coal mines or expansions.[102] The hypocrisy is breathtaking.

The same applies to Australia's stated commitment to the "international rules-based order". In January 2025, the Australian Defence Minister was asked if Australia would support Trump's attacks on the foundations of international law, perhaps a unilateral takeover of Panama, or annexation of Greenland. The best response Defence Minister Richard Marles could muster was that "our alliance with the US is really the cornerstone of our national security, our foreign policy".[103] No one in the current government is able to say that such a move — or a US "take over" of Gaza, for that matter — would be a clear breach of the international rule of law. It is extraordinary that a Labor government refuses to state unapologetically that Australia has a longstanding, and continuing, commitment to the institutions and structures of international law and that it is in both our and our closest ally's interests that that system survives. We are choosing to forgo our responsibility to protect and uphold the rule of law, to accept the significant risks to our security keeping Donald Trump on our side. Sometimes, as Phillip Coorey wrote in the *Australian Financial Review* in early 2024, "cosying up to a madman" is "a necessity".[104] Self-harm is never a necessity.

What kind of security is that? What do we think security actually *is*?

As Trump sets about dismantling what is left of the international rules-based order, destabilises the US and global economies, undermines public health, increases already rising inequality, unleashes white supremacy at home and abroad, accelerates catastrophic climate change — exactly as he told us he would — we need a better answer to that question. And we need it quickly.

We can and we must think about our security differently.

Real security is more than just the temporary prevention of war. In Australia, and across much of the Western world, foreign and security policy is built on the assumption that war is inevitable. This assumption is based on a selective understanding of history and of human behaviour that ends up reinforcing, rather than challenging, the worst trends in international relations. Pundits and politicians then make claims like "we live in the worst strategic circumstances since World War II", that we face a "new Cold War", that "great power competition" is necessary and completely beyond our control, without ever facing much challenge. Anyone who disagrees can be dismissed as an "appeaser".

Those historical analogies are appealing and comforting, because the world is a dangerous place. But that isn't how history works, and all those assumptions do is let those in power off the hook for their actions (or inactions). The suggestion that we face the worst strategic circumstances since the last global war, for example, implies that it doesn't matter what we do. In our circumstances, it suggests that our latest existential enemy is coming for us because that is what great powers do, and all we can do is prepare for the worst. That is the basic assumption of the ANZUS Treaty and Australian foreign and security policy more broadly; Australia is always threatened by enemies from the north. Those enemies don't look like us, and the only way we can protect ourselves from them is to fall in line behind another great (white) power. That, in the end, is what AUKUS is all about. AUKUS was, as it was described at the time, always about the revival of the Anglosphere. It is the fatalism that induces paralysis.

Both the United States and Australia often behave as if the provocative behaviour of the Anglosphere has nothing to do with how other nations respond. Any perception of Chinese aggression is framed as unreasonable and threatening. Anything that Australia does — such as embarking on a plan to acquire nuclear-powered submarines clearly designed to engage in conflict far from Australian shores — is necessary and self-evidently defensive.

China is, undoubtedly, a risk to be managed. But it is not a direct, immediate threat to Australia, and it is not inevitable that it will become one. Diplomacy, genuine engagement, cultural exchange, people-to-people contact: these are all tools available to us, tools that Australia has been historically good at using when we have chosen to.[105]

That genuine engagement — real relationships — requires a clear understanding of what our interests and values truly are. Right now, our approach to the world is undermined by the way our foreign and defence policy, and our alliance with the United States, actively contradict those values. Both Australia and the United States pride themselves on their democracies, on their democratic values. China is, rightly or wrongly, regarded as an existential enemy because it is *not* a democracy. And yet the way Australia approaches our engagement with China in the world is a very, very long way from democratic.

Australian foreign and security policy is marked by intense secrecy. AUKUS is the epitome of this practice: it was conceived entirely in secret and sprung on the Australian people overnight without any consultation. It still has not been subject to any serious parliamentary or democratic scrutiny. This is how critical decisions about national security are made in this country: in secret, mostly by men in suits or uniforms, with no democratic accountability. The AUKUS deal probably would not have survived independent, democratic scrutiny from Treasury, or Defence, at least not in its current form. But foreign and security policy in this country isn't subject to that kind of accountability, which results in unnecessary and eye-wateringly expensive agreements such as AUKUS. Agreements that do not make us safer; agreements that fundamentally misunderstand what does threaten us and thus dramatically increase our insecurity.

Secrecy does not create security. Secrecy undermines security, as it undermines democracy.

And these kinds of secretive deals also undermine what we are often told are the "shared democratic values" of our alliance with the United States. As AUKUS shows, the alliance is actively anti-democratic, and it is very far from transparent. An alliance with the United States that genuinely valued transparency, and democracy, would look very different. It wouldn't allow the revenge fantasies of men like Boris Johnson to dictate the future of our security, and the ability of future Australian governments to make independent decisions in the national interest. It wouldn't allow our closest ally to persecute an Australian citizen for publishing the truth.[106] It wouldn't allow for the punishment of whistleblowers and publishers exposing war crimes, as the only people to be punished for war crimes committed in the name of that alliance. It would value the truth. It would value transparency. These are things we can aspire to in Australian foreign policy that would make us more secure. It's not inevitable that we go without. It is entirely possible for Australia to reform our secrecy and whistleblower laws. In a democracy, we all have a right to contribute and to hold our leaders accountable for their decisions and actions.

A healthy democracy is built on the understanding that human security is the wellspring of national security. Human security — real, lasting security — means addressing inequality, building prosperity, acting on climate and protecting the environment on which we depend.

Australia has considerable power and agency, more than enough to pursue this kind of security. We are a rich country. We have the 13th largest economy in the world. When that world is on fire, we could choose to focus on fighting the flames instead of fanning them. Instead of spending upwards of $368 billion on escalatory military hardware, we could invest in things that make us safer. That could involve simple, practical choices.

As of early 2024, for example, Australia

had a fleet of just six large fixed-wing air tankers, 15 large helicopters, 70 medium and small helicopters, 56 small fixed-wing firebombers, and 15 light fixed-wing aircraft available for firefighting. Most of that fleet is privately owned; the government leases them as required. Annual government spending on this fleet totals around $125 million.[107] Over a 30-year period — the same delivery timeline imagined for the AUKUS deal — that's about $3.75 billion. Put another way, that amounts to about one per cent of the AUKUS budget. That it seems so unrealistic or even unreasonable to suggest that we might spend that kind of money on firefighting equipment instead of weapons is a marker of our current politics. But what would actually make us safer?

Investment in that kind of security is something we could do. We could decide, like Norway, that instead of charging our kids to go to university and subsidising fossil fuels to the tune of $14 billion, we could instead tax fossil fuels and make university free.[108] We could invest in public education, in public health, and action on climate change. We could operate in genuine partnership with countries in our region to build collective security.

As the former Treasurer Josh Frydenberg said when asked about the eye-watering amount of money his government had committed to AUKUS: "everything is affordable if it's a priority".[109]

None of that means abandoning our relationship with the United States. It does mean that relationship must change. We can rebalance and reprioritise that relationship away from its blind focus on a hollow understanding of "security" towards a genuine democratic solidarity. Australia can seek out, and support, those with an interest in the revival of American democracy, in Congress, in the courts, and in civil society. We can try to be the kind of friend that brings out the best in someone and pushes back on their worst instincts. The kind of friend that rejects demands for blind fealty. A real friend.

We, and the rest of the world along with us, have choices, power, and agency. We do not have to weather whatever Trump's America throws at us, hoping in vain for rare and costly scraps of his benevolence. As the Board of the Doomsday Clock explained in early 2025, we are in this situation precisely because "despite unmistakable signs of danger, national leaders and their societies have failed to do what is needed to change course".[110]

Disaster is not inevitable. Nothing is. We are capable of doing things differently from how we have done them before. We could play a leadership role in building genuine global security, by acting on climate change, on nuclear non-proliferation, on peacebuilding, and on safeguarding the international rule of law. Instead, we consistently underestimate and undermine our own influence by refusing to acknowledge what we have and refusing to consider what we might do with it. We could continue to choose irrelevance, or subservience, or we could choose something else. We could choose to continue with our usual meaningless and cowardly gestures towards a kind of "national security" that is, in reality, no security at all. Or we could choose another world. We could build a vision and a plan, together, for what this country and the world might look like after America. And that post-America world is coming whether we like it or not.

What Australia does matters. Our choices matter. We can choose to build a world after America. A world that is better and safer than the one we had before.

Endnotes

1 Dans and Groves (eds) (2023) *Mandate for Leadership: The Conservative Promise*

2 Lotz (2025) "'L.A. fires could be the U.S.' worst natural disaster', Newsom says,", https://www.axios.com/2025/01/12/la-wildfires-gavin-newsom-natural-disaster

3 Stelloh et al. (2025) "California wildfires: What we know about L.A.-area fires, what caused them, who is affected and more", https://www.nbcnews.com/news/us-news/california-wildfires-what-we-know-palisades-eaton-los-angeles-rcna188239

4 Governor Newsom (2025) Governor Newsom on Response to Palisades Fire in Southern California, https://x.com/CAgovernor/status/1876826666296848873; Climate Council (2025) "This is the climate crisis in action": hot, dry conditions fuel winter LA fires, https://www.climatecouncil.org.au/resources/climate-crisis-in-action-hot-dry-conditions-fuel-winter-la-fires/#:~:text=Californian%20Governor%20Gavin%20Newsom%20said,year%2C"%20Governor%20Newsom%20said

5 Bryant (2024) *Forever War*; Watson (2024) *High Noon*; Cooke (2019) *Tired of Winning*; Lepore (2018) *These Truths*

6 The Australia Institute (2025) "Poll: Trump a greater threat to world peace than Putin or Xi", https://australiainstitute.org.au/post/poll-trump-a-greater-threat-to-world-peace-than-putin-or-xi/

7 Ortolan (2025) "Los Angeles is burning, so how well prepared is Australia's aerial firefighting fleet?", https://www.abc.net.au/news/2025-01-14/australias-water-bombing-firefighting-fleet-explained/104811830

8 Lashof (2024) "Tracking Progress: Climate Action Under the Biden Administration", https://www.wri.org/insights/biden-administration-tracking-climate-action-progress

9 Irfan (2024) "Joe Biden's enormous, contradictory, and fragile climate legacy", https://www.vox.com/climate/362478/joe-biden-climate-change-legacy

10 Evans (2021) "Which countries are historically responsible for climate change?", https://www.carbonbrief.org/analysis-which-countries-are-historically-responsible-for-climate-change/

11 Peterson (2024) "U.S. crude oil production established a new record in August 2024", https://www.eia.gov/todayinenergy/detail.php?id=63824; Kriel (2024), "United States produces more crude oil than any country, ever", https://www.eia.gov/todayinenergy/detail.php?id=61545

12 U.S. Energy Information Administration (2025) "Natural Gas", https://www.eia.gov/dnav/ng/hist/n9050us2a.html; U.S. Energy Information Administration (2025) "Short-Term Energy Outlook" https://www.eia.gov/outlooks/steo/report/natgas.phpShort-Term Energy Outlook

13 Cameron (2025) "NOAA Employees Told to Pause Work With 'Foreign Nationals'", https://www.wired.com/story/noaa-employees-foreign-nationals/ /

14 Knickmeyer et al. (2025) "Trump administration says it's cutting 90% of USAID foreign aid contracts", https://apnews.com/article/trump-usaid-foreign-aid-cuts-6292f48f8d4025bed0bf-5c3e9d623c16Supreme

15 Karas (2025) "Shock and fear for food programs amid US aid freeze", https://www.devex.com/news/devex-dish-shock-and-fear-for-food-programs-amid-us-aid-freeze-109199

16 Harter (2025) "'The impact has been devastating': how USAID freeze sent shockwaves through Ethiopia", https://www.theguardian.com/global-development/ng-interactive/2025/feb/21/the-impact-has-been-devastating-how-usaid-freeze-sent-shockwaves-through-ethiopia

17 Hassoun (2025) "USAID's apparent demise and the US withdrawal from WHO put millions of lives worldwide at risk and imperil US national security", https://theconversation.com/usaids-apparent-demise-and-the-us-withdrawal-from-who-put-millions-of-lives-worldwide-at-risk-and-imperil-us-national-security-249260

18 Glenza (2025) "Trump's health department cancels meetings and pauses communications", https://www.theguardian.com/us-news/2025/jan/23/trump-health-department; Maxmen (2025) "What a US exit from the WHO means for global healthcare", https://www.aljazeera.com/news/2025/1/28/what-a-us-exit-from-the-who-means-for-global-healthcare

19 Human Rights Watch (2025) https://www.hrw.org/news/2025/02/05/trump-indicates-intent-escalate-ethnic-cleansing-gaza

20 Eco (1995) "Ur-Fascism", https://theanarchistlibrary.org/library/umberto-eco-ur-fascism

21 Gyngell (2018) *Fear of Abandonment: Australia in the World since 1942*

22 Albanese and Rowland (2024) "Press Conference — Parliament House, Canberra Transcript", https://www.pm.gov.au/media/press-conference-parliament-house-canberra-31

23 Marles (2025) "Great to speak with US Secretary of Defense", https://x.com/RichardMarlesMP/status/1884411140693975510

24 Helmore (2024) "Trump defense secretary nominee Pete Hegseth's mother called him 'an abuser of women'", https://www.theguardian.com/us-news/2024/nov/30/trump-defense-secretary-pick-pete-hegseth-mother-abuser-of-women

25 Marles (2025) "Opening Remarks, Meeting with US Secretary of Defense, Washington DC", https://www.minister.defence.gov.au/transcripts/2025-02-08/opening-remarks-meeting-us-secretary-defense-washington-dc

26 Marles (2025) "Opening Remarks, Meeting with US Secretary of Defense, Washington DC"

27 Koziol (2025) "Deposit paid: Trump 'very aware' of AUKUS as Marles hands over $800m", https://www.smh.com.au/world/north-america/deposit-paid-trump-very-aware-of-aukus-as-marles-hands-over-800m-20250208-p5lajg.html

28 Grattan (2025) "Trump agrees to consider Australian exemption from tariffs, describing

Albanese as 'very fine man'", https://theconversation.com/trump-agrees-to-consider-australian-exemption-from-tariffs-describing-albanese-as-very-fine-man-248886

29 Vyas (2025) "'Donald Trump's what does that mean?' AUKUS remark played down as verbal slip-up", https://www.abc.net.au/news/2025-02-28/donald-trump-asks-what-aukus-means-after-keir-starmer-meeting/104993110

30 Hegseth (2025) "Opening Remarks by Secretary of Defense Pete Hegseth at Ukraine Defense Contact Group (As Delivered)", https://www.defense.gov/News/Speeches/Speech/Article/4064113/opening-remarks-by-secretary-of-defense-pete-hegseth-at-ukraine-defense-contact/

31 Ross (2025) "Playbook PM: Vance delivers a gut punch to Europe", https://www.politico.com/newsletters/playbook-pm/2025/02/14/vance-delivers-a-gut-punch-to-europe-00132333

32 Behm (2024) "The Doomed Political Conceit of AUKUS", https://www.theaustralian.com.au/special-reports/the-doomed-conceit-of-a-political-aukus/news-story/996bdefa821b03c6559b51c1a3286b26

33 Congressional Research Service (2025) "Navy Virginia-Class Submarine Program and AUKUS Submarine (Pillar 1) Project: Background and Issues for Congress", https://crsreports.congress.gov/product/pdf/RL/RL32418/287; Green and McClaren (2024) "Congressional report suggests Australia could dump plans to acquire AUKUS nuclear submarines", https://www.abc.net.au/news/2024-10-17/

report-suggests-australia-dump-aukus-nuclear-submarine-plans/104486868

34 Australian Government Defence (2023) "AUKUS nuclear-powered submarine pathway", www.minister.defence.gov.au/media-releases/2023-03-14/aukus-nuclear-powered-submarine-pathway

35 Armitage (2021) "Joe Biden calls Scott Morrison 'that fella Down Under' during AUKUS nuclear submarine announcement", https://www.abc.net.au/news/2021-09-16/joe-biden-calls-scott-morrison-fella-down-under/100466514

36 Marles (2023) "Address to the National Press Club", https://www.minister.defence.gov.au/speeches/2023-11-28/address-national-press-club

37 Australian Government Australian Submarine Agency (n.d.) "Collins Class submarines", https://www.asa.gov.au/aukus/collins-class-submarines .

38 Salisbury (2023) "The Sinking Submarine Industrial Base", https://warontherocks.com/2023/10/the-sinking-submarine-industrial-base/

39 Sabbagh (2021) "Trident nuclear submarine replacement delayed by another year", https://www.theguardian.com/uk-news/2021/feb/04/trident-nuclear-submarine-replacement-delayed-by-year; Briggs (2024) AUKUS: A solution to the risky UK gambit, https://www.lowyinstitute.org/the-interpreter/aukus-solution-risky-uk-gambit

40 Hurst (2024) "Australia risks being 'world's nuclear waste dump' unless Aukus laws changed, critics say", https://www.theguardian.com/world/article/2024/may/13/australia-aukus-deal-submarines-critics-nuclear-waste

41 Curran (2024) "Senior US diplomat lets the AUKUS

cat out of the bag", https://www.afr.com/policy/foreign-affairs/senior-us-diplomat-lets-the-aukus-cat-out-of-the-bag-20240407-p5fhyt

42 United States Institute of Peace (2021) "Beyond AUKUS and the Quad: What's Next for the U.S. Indo-Pacific Strategy", https://www.usip.org/events/beyond-aukus-and-quad-whats-next-us-indo-pacific-strategy https://www.usip.org/events/beyond-aukus-and-quad-whats-next-us-indo-pacific-strategy

43 Marles (2022) "Address to the US Center for Strategic and International Studies", https://www.themandarin.com.au/194438-richard-marles-address-to-the-us-center-for-strategic-and-international-studies/ -international-studies/

44 Tillett (2024) "AUKUS chiefs torpedo submarine sales fears", https://www.afr.com/politics/federal/aukus-chiefs-torpedo-submarine-sales-fears-20240830-p5k6mj

45 Shortis (2021) *Our Exceptional Friend*

46 Feast and Kelly (2021) "'Inconceivable' Australia would not join U.S. to defend Taiwan — Australian defence minister", https://www.reuters.com/world/asia-pacific/inconceivable-australia-would-not-join-us-defend-taiwan-australian-defence-2021-11-12/ /

47 Karp (2023) "Labor thrashes out Aukus position at party conference amid dissent from MP and unions", https://www.theguardian.com/australia-news/2023/aug/18/alp-national-conference-labor-aukus-position-unions-mp-anthony-albanese

48 Biden (2022) "Remarks on Democracy", https://www.c-span.org/video/?c5029494/president-biden-inflection-point

49 Mecklin (2025) "2025 Doomsday Clock Statement", https://thebulletin.org/doomsday-clock/2025-statement/ https://thebulletin.org/doomsday-clock/2025-statement/

50 The White House (n.d.) https://obamawhitehouse.archives.gov/node/360106

51 Biden (2020) "US president-elect Joe Biden claims victory", https://www.abc.net.au/news/2020-11-08/us-president-elect-joe-biden-victory-speech-full-transcript/12861698

52 Shortis (2023) "With US trip, PM Albanese flies into the light", https://australiainstitute.org.au/post/with-us-trip-pm-albanese-flies-into-the-light/ /

53 Byrne and Shortis (2025) "Joe Biden's presidency will be remembered as one that did not match the times, and a leader who failed to realise it", https://theconversation.com/joe-bidens-presidency-will-be-remembered-as-one-that-did-not-match-the-times-and-a-leader-who-failed-to-realise-it-246320 0

54 Congress (2021) "Summary: H.R.4346 — 117th Congress (2021-2022)", https://www.congress.gov/bill/117th-congress/house-bill/4346 https://www.congress.gov/bill/117th-congress/house-bill/4346

55 State Department (2025) https://www.state.gov/bureau-of-political-military-affairs/releases/2025/01/u-s-security-cooperation-with-ukraine

56 Ward (2023) "'Rock solid and unwavering': Biden pledges support for Israel after Hamas attacks", https://www.politico.com/news/2023/10/07/hamas-terrorism-attacks-on-israeli-civilians-00120480 0

57 O'Toole (2020) "Designated Mourner with appropriate fawning", https://www.nybooks.com/

articles/2020/01/16/joe-biden-designated-mourner/
58 Ward (2023) "'Rock solid and unwavering': Biden pledges support for Israel after Hamas attacks"
59 Watson Institute for International and Public Affairs (2023) "United States Spending on Israel's Military Operations and Related U.S. Operations in the Region, October 7, 2023–September 30, 2024", https://watson.brown.edu/costsofwar/papers/2024/USspendingIsrael
60 Masters and Merrow (2024) "U.S. Aid to Israel in Four Charts", https://www.cfr.org/article/us-aid-israel-four-charts
61 Behm, Shortis, Bowker (2025) "Beyond the Two State Solution", https://australiainstitute.org.au/report/beyond-the-two-state-solution/
62 Duss and Okail (2024) "America is Cursed by Foreign Policy Nostalgia", https://www.foreignaffairs.com/united-states/america-cursed-foreign-policy-nostalgia
63 Taylor (2025) "Labor was warned its perceived 'one-sided' Israel support over Gaza raised social cohesion concerns", https://www.theguardian.com/australia-news/2025/mar/10/labor-australia-government-israel-gaza-social-cohesion-ntwnfb
64 Gabbatt (2024) "'In America, it's viewed as too extreme': self-immolation as protest — and sacrifice", https://www.theguardian.com/us-news/2024/mar/04/self-immolation-protest-sacrifice
65 Leingang (2024) "How the uncommitted movement rocked Biden over Gaza", https://www.theguardian.com/us-news/2024/mar/17/us-uncommitted-voters-biden-gaza
66 Watson Institute for International and Public

Affairs (2021) "Human and Budgetary Costs to Date of the U.S. War in Afghanistan, 2001–2022", https://watson.brown.edu/costsofwar/figures/2021/human-and-budgetary-costs-date-us-war-afghanistan-2001–2022

67 Tressie McMillan Cottom (2019) *Thick and Other Essays*

68 Harris (2024) "Full Concession Speech", https://time.com/7173617/kamala-harris-concession-speech-full-transcript/

69 Duss (2025) "Democrats have become the party of war. Americans are tired of it", https://www.theguardian.com/us-news/ng-interactive/2025/jan/09/democrats-war-foreign-policy

70 NBC News (2024) "'If somebody breaks in my house, they're getting shot,' Harris tells Oprah", https://www.nbcnews.com/video/-if-somebody-breaks-in-my-house-they-re-getting-shot-harris-tells-oprah-219779653904

71 Duss (2025) "Democrats have become the party of war. Americans are tired of it"

72 Kronengberg (2024) "How Many People Didn't Vote in the 2024 Election?", https://www.usnews.com/news/national-news/articles/2024-11-15/how-many-people-didnt-vote-in-the-2024-election

73 Watson (2024) *High Noon*

74 The White House (2019) "Remarks by President Trump and Prime Minister Morrison of Australia at Arrival Ceremony", https://trumpwhitehouse.archives.gov/briefings-statements/remarks-president-trump-prime-minister-morrison-australia-arrival-ceremony/

75 Griffiths et al. (2017) "US military defends dropping

'mother of all bombs' on ISIS in Afghanistan", https://edition.cnn.com/2017/04/14/asia/afghanistan-isis-moab-bomb https://edition.cnn.com/2017/04/14/asia/afghanistan-isis-moab-bomb

76 Wright (2017) "Trump Drops the Mother of All Bombs on Afghanistan", https://www.newyorker.com/news/news-desk/trump-drops-the-mother-of-all-bombs-on-afghanistan https://www.newyorker.com/news/news-desk/trump-drops-the-mother-of-all-bombs-on-afghanistan

77 Butterworth (2019) "Donald Trump threatens Afghanistan that he could wipe it 'off the face of the Earth'", https://www.abc.net.au/news/2019-07-25/why-did-donald-trump-say-he-could-kill-10-million-afghans/11342794

78 Crowley, Hassem, Schmidt (2020) "U.S. Strike in Iraq Kills Qassim Suleimani, Commander of Iranian Forces", https://www.nytimes.com/2020/01/02/world/middleeast/qassem-soleimani-iraq-iran-attack.html

79 Shortis (2019) *Our Exceptional Friend*

80 Van Jackson (2018) *On the Brink: Trump, Kim, and the Threat of Nuclear War*

81 Shortis, Mitchell (2024) "The worm kingdom", https://omny.fm/shows/after-america/the-worm-kingdom https://australiainstitute.org.au/post/the-worm-kingdom/Mitchell

82 Lopez (2025) "Hegseth Tells NATO Hard Power Provides Deterrence, Defense", https://www.defense.gov/News/News-Stories/Article/Article/4066810/hegseth-tells-nato-hard-power-provides-deterrence-defense/

83 Hegseth (2024) *The War on Warriors*

84 Quincy Inst Conference (2024) "What a Foreign Policy For the Middle Class Looks Like: Realism and Restraint Amid Global Conflict", https://quincyinst.s3.amazonaws.com/wp-content/uploads/2024/05/28124444/TRANSCRIPT-5.23-QI-Conference.docx.pdf

85 Goldenberg (2003) "US defends role for evangelical christians", https://www.theguardian.com/world/2003/oct/17/religion.uk2; Suskind (2004) "Faith, Certainty and the Presidency of George W. Bush", https://www.nytimes.com/2004/10/17/magazine/faith-certainty-and-the-presidency-of-george-w-bush.html Something about Bush Jr?

86 Olmos (2022) "'Key to white survival': how Putin has morphed into a far-right savior", https://www.theguardian.com/us-news/2022/mar/05/putin-ukraine-invasion-white-nationalists-far-right

87 Hegseth (2025) "Opening Remarks by Secretary of Defense Pete Hegseth at Ukraine Defense Contact Group (As Delivered)", https://www.defense.gov/News/Speeches/Speech/Article/4064113/opening-remarks-by-secretary-of-defense-pete-hegseth-at-ukraine-defense-contact/

88 The Heritage Foundation (2023) *Mandate for Leadership: The Conservative Promise*

89 Shortis (2024) "Project 2025, the policy substance behind Trump's showmanship, reveals a radical plan to reshape the world", https://theconversation.com/friday-essay-project-2025-the-policy-substance-behind-trumps-showmanship-reveals-a-radical-plan-to-reshape-the-world-227161

90 Green and Solender (2025) "Scoop: Dems pissed at liberal groups MoveOn, Indivisible",

https://www.axios.com/2025/02/12/democrats-jeffries-move-on-indivisible-trump
91 Howell (2024) "Labour's Historic Victory Belies Deep Fault Lines in British Politics", https://www.thenation.com/article/world/labour-uk-election-victory/
92 Chase (2024) "Inside Trudeau's Mar-a-Lago dinner with Trump — and how it all went down", https://www.theglobeandmail.com/politics/article-donald-trump-dinner-justin-trudeau-mar-a-lago/
93 Polling Canada (2025) "Last two Liberal data points are with Carney as leader", https://x.com/CanadianPolling/status/1891950219127857280
94 Wike et al. (2024) "Representative Democracy Remains a Popular Ideal, but People Around the World Are Critical of How It's Working", https://www.pewresearch.org/global/2024/02/28/representative-democracy-remains-a-popular-ideal-but-people-around-the-world-are-critical-of-how-its-working/
95 The Australia Institute (2024) "Stage 3 Tax Cuts and Election Promises", https://australiainstitute.org.au/post/high-income-earners-coalition-voters-among-those-backing-stage-3-redesign/
96 Schmidt (2024) "Here's what Harris and Trump said about climate change", https://whyy.org/articles/election-2024-presidential-debate-climate-change/
97 Thrower (2024) "Yes, the government collects more money from HECS than it does from the petroleum resource rent tax", https://australiainstitute.org.au/post/yes-the-government-collects-more-money-from-hecs-than-it-does-from-the-petroleum-resource-rent-tax/
98 Behm (2024) *The Odd Couple: the Australia–America*

relationship

99 Trump (2019) "Remarks by President Trump and Prime Minister Morrison of Australia at State Dinner", https://trumpwhitehouse.archives.gov/briefings-statements/remarks-president-trump-prime-minister-morrison-australia-state-dinner/

100 The Australia Institute (2025) "Poll: Trump a greater threat to world peace than Putin or Xi", https://australiainstitute.org.au/post/poll-trump-a-greater-threat-to-world-peace-than-putin-or-xi/

101 Campbell et al. (2024) "Fossil fuel subsidies in Australia 2024", https://australiainstitute.org.au/report/fossil-fuel-subsidies-in-australia-2024/

102 The Australia Institute (n.d.) "Coal Mine Tracker", https://australiainstitute.org.au/initiative/coal-mine-tracker/ https://australiainstitute.org.au/initiative/coal-mine-tracker/.

103 Marles (2025) https://www.minister.defence.gov.au/transcripts/2025-03-05/radio-interview-5aa-mornings

104 Coorey (2024) "Indiscreet Rudd has only himself to blame for Trump outburst", https://www.afr.com/politics/federal/indiscreet-rudd-only-has-himself-to-blame-for-trump-outburst-20240320-p5fds1

105 Curran (2022) *Australia's China Odyssey: From Euphoria to Fear*

106 Shortis (2024) "Julian Assange saga was straining Australia–US alliance", https://www.abc.net.au/news/2024-06-26/julian-assange-saga-was-straining-australia-us/104023330

107 Home Affairs Portfolio Parliament of Australia (2024) "More aircraft to keep Australians safer from disasters", https://minister.homeaffairs.gov.au/

MurrayWatt/Pages/more-aircraft-keep-australians-safer-from-disasters.aspx

108 The Australia Institute (2024) "Explainer: How the government collects more from HECS/HELP than the PRRT", https://australiainstitute.org.au/post/explainer-how-Explainer: How the- government-collects- more- from-hecs-help- HECS/HELP than- the-prrt/

109 Hartcher (2022) "Radioactive: Inside the top-secret AUKUS subs deal", https://www.smh.com.au/politics/federal/radioactive-inside-the-top-secret-aukus-subs-deal-20220510-p5ak7g.html

110 Mecklin (2025) "2025 Doomsday Clock Statement", https://thebulletin.org/doomsday-clock/2025-statement/

Acknowledgements

My deepest thanks, as always, go to Allan Behm. Thank you also to generous and thoughtful readers in Richard Denniss, Don Watson, Richard Cooke and Frank Yuan, and to Pritika Kumar for editorial support. Thank you to Angus Blackman, who built this concept with me. But most of all, thank you to Alice Grundy, who is patient, and kind, and a wonderful editor.

About the author

Dr Emma Shortis is Director of The Australia Institute's International & Security Affairs Program. Emma's first book, *Our Exceptional Friend: Australia's Fatal Alliance with the United States*, was published by Hardie Grant in 2021. She writes regularly for Australian and international outlets, appears regularly on Australian radio and television and hosts the podcast, *After America*.

Before joining The Australia Institute, Emma was a Lecturer at RMIT University, where her academic work focused on international relations and climate transition. She spent a year in the United States as Fox-Zucker International Fellow at Yale University, where she finished her PhD in History.

About The Australia Institute

The Australia Institute conducts research that drives the public debate and secures policy outcomes to make Australia better.
The Australia Institute's independence and non-partisanship ensures our work is guided by a vision for a fairer Australia, without political or commercial influence. Our research regularly calls into question powerful vested interests, multinational corporations, and the economic orthodoxy.

This work is only possible because of independent donations. The support of our donors powers the Institute's ability to fulfill its motto: research that matters. To contribute to our work and ongoing research, you can make a donation on our website by scanning the QR code below.

Vantage Point: Issue 1

Read it and pass it on. Put your name and email below and start a conversation with other readers.

Name	Contact